Holy Spirit Feed Me

100 Days of Fasting

Uncle Lawrence,

Thanks for being
a cool uncle -
Blessings!

Ulysses Lopez

Preface

My iPhone alarm goes off at 4:15 a.m. on Easter Sunday and I hit the snooze button twice before getting out of bed. I've decided to sign up and volunteer at the Charlotte Rescue Mission to help serve the homeless. I've also decided to begin a spiritual fast for the next hundred days and not eat anything—no snacks, not one meal. However, I will partake in communion. The point of the fast is to become closer to God and build a stronger relationship with Him; I believe communion will help me.

A hundred days from now is the 4th of July. That's a lot of grilling I'm going to miss out on. On the other hand, this could be the most impactful event of my life. I've fasted in the past—my longest is forty-five days. A lot of prayers were answered during that period. The results were amazing. I lost sixty pounds and I've never felt better.

Now I live in Charlotte, North Carolina and I've been here for almost a year. The change has been significant but positive. I quit my sales job, I'm closer to family and back on the east coast, and I've been accepted into Montreat College's Clinical Mental Health Counseling Program. I want to become a licensed professional counselor and help people. I can empathize and I have compassion for those suffering in their life, because I've overcome many obstacles myself. My life experiences, although challenging, have been rewarding.

I served in the army for eight years and was deployed to Iraq twice. I have seen what war does to soldiers and how the experience adversely affects their life. I know because it severely affected mine. I treated myself with sex, drugs, and alcohol, but nothing worked. I had moments where the sex and alcohol would numb the pain, but only for a short time. My life only improved after I recommitted my life to Jesus Christ on December 18, 2011. I also dumped all the medication, given to me by the Veterans Affairs (VA) Outpatient Clinic, down the toilet. The VA gave me all types of pills without understanding me or what I was going through. The many disingenuous experiences at the VA have induced me to find a healthier solution to deal with issues like anxiety, depression, and post-traumatic stress disorder, or PTSD.

I didn't know much about fasting or spiritual fasts until Christmas 2012. I spent Christmas at my grandparents' home in Summerville, South Carolina. My grandmother always has Christian books to share with me. This time, she handed me a book Pastor Jentezen Franklin wrote on fasting. I read the book in two sittings and grew fascinated with the concept. Jentezen Franklin is the first pastor who I've heard expound on it.

Part of being a Christian is praying, giving, and fasting. So many Christian pastors speak about the first two and leave out the latter. I began to research the concept—how it brings you closer to God as it breaks you away from the world. I came across Pastor Rick Warren's book, which spoke of a form of fasting called the Daniel Fast. I really liked his book and how Daniel (a character in the Bible) removed certain foods from his diet and became stronger in the Lord—he became an overcomer.

I also researched the health benefits of a variety of fruits and vegetables and learned that they can heal the body. At that time, I lived in Austin, Texas, and living a healthy lifestyle is easy in Austin. There are juice bars all over the city. My favorite juice spot in Austin is Juiceland. They have a juice that tastes like a peanut butter and jelly sandwich.

Since 2012, I've been juice fasting on and off. I'm adamant about the health benefits and the spiritual breakthrough that results. Toward the end of 2015, I knew I was going to start 2016 with a fast. I felt the Lord was speaking to me. I felt as though he wanted me to do a long fast and really purge my body of all toxins, literally and figuratively. I have broken away from toxic people, toxic music, and a toxic environment. As I grow closer to the Lord, I have become more sensitive to the Holy Spirit. I can sense good and evil and want to stay clear of all evil.

Breaking away from the world is challenging. I tried to begin this hundred-day fast on January 1, 2016 but failed. I tried once more on January 10th and failed yet again. I have attempted this hundred-day fast for the past two-and-a-half months and failed. It's not easy. But I decided to keep praying about it and I was led by the Lord to begin this fast on Easter Sunday. I counted a hundred days on the calendar and that will take me to July 4th. I'm also going to keep this fast as confidential as possible. I want to write my down my experiences, the daily Bible verses I'm reading, and what juices I'm making. I'm excited to start this hundred-day journey. I can't wait to see what the Lord reveals to me and what type of breakthroughs I will have.

Day 1

Juice: kale, pineapple, strawberries, grapes, raw honey
Bible verses: Proverb 1, Psalm 1-2
Weight: 287.5 lb

It's 4:45 a.m. and I'm driving to the Charlotte Rescue Mission. It has been raining all night and it's chilly outside. I made my juice, but left it on the kitchen counter. Thank goodness I at least took a swig before heading out. It's day one of my fast and so far, I'm not feeling any anxiety. I'm usually thinking about all the foods I'm missing out on—pizza, steaks, seafood, and cheeseburgers. I love cheeseburgers. I also love Wendy's dollar menu. The first day of a fast is always the hardest. In the past, it's usually on the first day itself that I fail a fast. I'll make it through the day, then the anxiety hits and I drive to Wendy's or McDonald's. I feel no shame in sharing this; it's part of the process.

I arrive at the Charlotte Rescue Mission. My only responsibility is to make the homeless feel welcomed and serve them breakfast. The Charlotte Rescue Mission is really helping the homeless and I'm happy to be a volunteer. God called us all to serve. Jesus was an ambassador for the poor. It's Easter Sunday and I'm serving. Today, this is my church.

I still feel good on day one. I met a lot of nice people while volunteering today. It's important I know my community. Even though I'm conversing with others, my fast is on my mind. I really don't want to screw this up. I'm adamant about starting this fast on Easter.

My volunteering duty is complete and it's time for me to leave. I'm tired; I've been awake since 4:15 a.m. and I'm beginning to feel worn out from the fast. It beats being anxious and giving up. I flop on my comfortable bed and fall asleep immediately. Day one is over. Thank God, I made it.

Day 2

Juice: kale, strawberries, banana, raw honey

Bible verses: Proverb 2, Psalm 3-4

Today feels surreal. I'm tired but not fatigued. I am able to go through my daily routine but slower. I'm waiting for the panic to hit and to fail this fast. I made it through the first day, but I'm not completely confident that I won't fail today. I'm going to take it easy so I don't burn too many calories and become hungry. I believe incorporating green tea will help. It will also help rid me of the toxins, while suppressing my hunger. I keep the blinds closed today; I don't want to see the outside world. My bed is so comfortable; I'm going to stay in bed and watch movies on my computer.

One of the Bible verses I read today, Proverbs 2, has a subheading, The Value of Wisdom. The purpose of this fast is partly to receive more wisdom from God.

It's easy to want more money, power, and respect, but wisdom is attained through understanding, intelligence, and education. I also believe being at peace will help me gain wisdom. One of my flaws is not being able to rest, let go, and let God. If I'm not working or keeping myself busy, I feel like I'm doing something wrong. I believe God wants me to rest right now and this fast will help slow down to a relaxed pace. It will slow down my thoughts, my words, and my steps. I need to learn to take it easy.

Day 3

Juice: kale, kiwi, pineapple, strawberries, raw honey, cinnamon
Bible verses: Proverb 3, Psalm 5-6

I made it another day and I'm surprised how easy this fast is going. I've made enough juice to last me all day. I bought a Blendtec WildSide blender and it's one of the best investments I've made this year. I use less fruits and vegetables and there is no waste, which is the best part.

I've been drinking about seventy-two ounces of juice a day. I blend all the ingredients in the morning and refrigerate it without removing it from the blender jar. When I want more juice, I pour it into my protein shaker. I use the protein shaker to shake it up.

I added cinnamon to my juice today. Cinnamon is a great spice, because it has so many added values. It's great to help cut the bitterness of the kale as well.

Today's juice is heavy with kale. I put a lot of kale, because I want to make sure I'm getting the nutrition I need from leafy green vegetables. Kale is an amazing superfood.

When I began juicing, I'd type "health benefits of . . ." into google. I'd read everything I could about the particular fruit or vegetable I'm research-ing and learn the benefits of mixing them together into a juice.

Juicing can be fun, because you're learning about the ingredients you eat and how they benefit your health and body without the need for medi-cation. We eat so many different foods, but we aren't always knowledgeable about their benefits. We have to teach ourselves about the foods we choose to put in our body. I am praying that tomorrow I feel stronger than today and that I wake up with a lot of energy.

Day 4

Juice: *kale, kiwi, grapes,s trawberries, banana*
Bible verses: *Proverb 4, Psalm 7–8*
Morning Exercise: *1 set of 15 reps: low row, triceps, and lat pulldown, biceps*
Weight: *282.1 lb, 5.4lb loss*

I feel great today! I woke up at 5:30 a.m. with an immediate burst of energy. I can't believe I feel this good and it's only day 4. I want to go to the gym, but I shouldn't: when I felt this great in the past, I would push myself too hard at the gym and then fail my fast, because I was so hungry and dizzy. This time, I'm going to soft-pedal through my gym routine. I still can't believe how good I feel. My body is filled with fruits and vegetables, and I feel really clean. I haven't had any headaches and my mind is alert. I believe this fast is anointed and I have God's hand on me. I've never felt like this before. I went to the gym and I only did one set of fifteen—enough so I could feel the burn, but not over-exert myself. I want to weigh myself only every Monday throughout this fast, but I feel light and I'm curious. I stepped on the scale and found I'm now 282.1 pounds. I lost 5.4 pounds and it's only day 4 of my fast. I know it's mainly water weight, but it's still five pounds.

I'm happy I have this energy, because I have an eventful day ahead of me. I am in an art therapy class for veterans and we meet every Wednesday afternoon. I decided to try out oil painting. I've only used acrylics in the past, so I'm new to oils. The class is awesome; everyone is friendly and most of the students are middle-aged and senior citizens. Everyone is talented as well and I'm learning a lot. Since I want to become a therapist, I took this class to learn about art therapy and its benefits.

My art teacher, Eileen Schwartz, gives me a quick lesson on using oils and two hours later, I complete a full painting. It's not the best but I'm proud of it. The painting is a sunset over the ocean with palm trees. In June, we are putting on an art exhibit called, Art by Vets. I've finished my first painting and I'm hooked. After class, I went home and ordered an easel so I can paint at home. The benefits are remarkable: I feel calm and relaxed. I believe we all feel good when we create something with our hands. I created something tangible today. Funny how one day can be so impactful. When I woke up this morning, I had no clue I was going to create a piece of art.

I think I'm really excited to get back to painting, because of the positive health benefits I received from it in the past. I haven't painted for a year since I moved from Austin. I love the focus it takes—how I can eliminate all of the distractions of life and just paint. I also know I need an outlet. In the past, my outlet was going to a bar. I don't want to go back to that lifestyle, ever. I try not to beat myself up about my past. I might have some dark moments, but I also have a lot of great moments.

I have traveled all over the world. I lived in Germany for three years. I went jet-skiing in the Dead Sea. I've been to the Louvre. I spent almost two years of my life in Iraq. I went to culinary school for a year, and know how to make amazing dishes. While living in Austin, I worked as an actor for a while as well. I've done a lot. I need to focus on those happy moments in my life and not let anyone steal my joy.

I really believe that as I shed weight, I'm shedding the hurts, the resentments, and the dark moments of my past. I will be a new creature. My body is a temple for God to live in. It's about time I make this body the best temple for Him to live in.

Day 5

Juice: *kale, spinach, apple, grapes*
Bible verses: *Proverb 5, Psalm 9-10*

It's gloomy outside and that's exactly how I feel. Yesterday I had so much energy, but today, I'm sluggish. I woke up and went directly to the couch to begin watching TV. I didn't move for a couple of hours. Mentally, I feel clear, but my body is fatigued again. I didn't make juice until 3 p.m. today. I'm beginning to sense my emotions are heightened; it's normal to become emotional during a fast. I'm feeling angry and frustrated, but I still experience moments of content and peace.

I hear a knock at my front door and I look out the peephole. Two members of my former church are standing outside. I left that church, because members of my life group don't respect boundaries and have made snide comments to me. Now, that same person is outside my door. Unbelievable. I completely understand why nonbelievers don't like Christians and why so many people don't like Jesus: a lot of Christians have given Jesus a bad reputation because of how they act. Hypocrites! Remove the plank from your eye before you try and remove the speck from mine. Jesus was a man of "no reputation" and some Christians have tried to ruin that aspect of him.

A lot of Christians don't realize we are all at different stages in our relationship with Christ. Making snide comments or judging one another shows a lack of maturity in one's walk with Christ. Some Christians need to stop talking so much and just listen. Now I have this guy outside my door. The leasing office calls to inform me that a member of my church is concerned about me and is coming over shortly to check up on me. Well, I'm fine. I'm sitting on my couch with my dog, watching the cooking channel. I refuse to answer the door. I hope he'll go away. I hope my day gets better.

Since I quit my sales job, I have a lot of time on my hands. I actually need this break and time to rest. I go to museums a lot and like the stillness and quiet of it. I love art. My eye is drawn to abstract art and impressionism. I want to go to the museum today, as well, but not the typical museum.

I don't know if it's the Lord moving me, but the Billy Graham Museum pops into my head.

The Billy Graham Museum is pretty cool; it's also free. When the tour begins, a talking cow gives you a brief background on Billy Graham. One of the last statements the cow makes is: "God can use anyone, even a farm boy from Charlotte, North Carolina." I feel the Holy Spirit hit me like a ton of bricks and become emotional. I had to actually hold back my tears. I feel ridiculous that this stupid talking cow almost made me cry. I continue on the tour, listening to Billy Graham preach on the screen and seeing all he has done to spread the word of God. No one can deny he is an impactful man. Billy Graham has met with world leaders, presidents, and entertainers. It's amazing to see how God really can use anybody. I'm praying the Lord uses me to help people, too. Becoming a therapist is important to me—so many people are hurting. We all have a common denominator: to be loved and accepted. I don't know how God is going to use me on this journey, but I do know He has used me in the past. He used me as a soldier and a sergeant in the army. A top sales representative at the marketing firm I worked at, He used me as a leader in my graduate cohort and somehow, He is using me on this fast. I try not to focus on just how the fast might benefit me but on what I can do to give back to the Lord.

Day 6

Juice: kale, spinach, apple, grapes

Bible verses: Proverb 6, Psalm 11-12

I had the same exact juice as yesterday, because I barely drank any juice today. I barely had any fluids and I'm tired; this week is going by slow. I'm also starting to have cabin fever. I quit my job two months ago. I know it sounds crazy, but I feel the Lord wanted me to give up sales and focus on school and on a life of helping others. The only problem is my resume does not reflect any of that.

I do have a lot of volunteer experience under my belt. I have volunteered for the Veterans Affairs Outpatient Clinic in Austin, TX. I've volunteered at different churches and even for music festivals. However, nothing reflects the career path of a licensed professional counselor. As the days turn into months, I feel like I am at Henry David Thoreau's Walden. My daily routine is becoming mundane and I'm fighting depression. Sometimes I feel like God is a fraternity brother, constantly hazing me to prove my loyalty. I understand why so many Christians backslide: it's not easy to have faith. It takes courage to have faith, and only brave people can trust and have faith in God.

In present society, it seems like most people are repulsed by the name of Jesus Christ. It's okay to claim God, but once you say Jesus Christ, the tables turn and some people become standoffish. It's sad. We all want to be loved and accepted, but so few give acceptance without judgment. You see this in all races and religions. Instead of shoving religion down people's throats, we need to get back to basics and first learn how to communicate with one another and listen to one another.

I do trust that God loves me, and all of what I'm going through will work in his favor as well as mine. I just need to vent and get it out. I don't have the luxury of relying on others. I live in Charlotte by myself. I'm neither married, nor have a girlfriend, nor too many people close to me. All I have is Top, my loyal German shepherd. I see God in Top a lot. He's the best dog I've ever been around and we've been together since he was ten weeks old. He's now a little over a year old. He's also a trained medical alert dog. He's highly intelligent and always by my side.

Even though I'm tired and depressed, I did have a peaceful day. My easel arrived today, so now I can paint at home. I went to the local art store and picked up a few oil brushes and a few other materials. I even received a check for a settlement that I didn't know anything about. This was a pleasant surprise. I do sometimes pray for unexpected income, so I had an answered prayer. The check is enough money to fill up my gas tank or buy groceries; it's not a lot but it's free money—who can complain about that? Maybe this is another one of God's tests. Can I thank Him for the little things and keep His name forever praised? In the middle of the storm, can I trust Him and know His power lives within me? It's easy to love God when life is filled with sunshine and rainbows. But can we love Him through the thunderstorms and hail showers? God has gotten me through the worst of times. I know this is just a season and something great will come out of this. In Psalm 46:10, the Lord says, "Be still and know that I am God." Being still is not easy for me. Being patient is almost torturous. Sometimes, it seems the simplest things in life—a wife, healthy kids, an impactful career, wealth, love—are the hardest to attain. However, God says in the rest of that same Bible verse: "I will be exalted among the nations, I will be exalted in the earth!" I need to focus on the latter portion of the verse.

Day 7

Juice: kale, spinach, apple, banana, strawberry, raw honey, organic peanut butter

Bible verses: *Proverb 7, Psalm 13-14*

I went to the grocery store today and picked up a few things. One item I picked up was organic peanut butter. The peanut butter I picked costs almost $6; for that price, it better be good.

I made my juice today and it was one of the best juices I've had during this fast and during prior fasts. The peanut butter really adds another layer of flavor.

I have a good amount of energy this morning. My thoughts are clear and my mind is focused. I decide not to work out at the gym but to stretch in the sauna and sit in the hot tub. The sauna helps to relieve stress and sweat out toxins; it feels good in the sauna; I get a good sweat going on. I shower off and head to the hot tub. The jet stream on my lower back feels great, but I'm beginning to feel light headed. I get out and head to the shower. I'm completely drained and fatigued. I thought I was going to pass out. I was planning on going to the Bechtel Museum of Modern Art after the gym, but now I'm too tired to go. I head home and my energy comes back.

The first week of fasting is such a rollercoaster. I thought by day seven I would have my energy back and feel refreshed, renewed, and recharged; so far, that's not the case. My energy is fickle and it's annoying. Today's another day of resting.

Day **8**

Juice: banana, grapes, apple, peanut butter
Bible verses: Proverb 8, Psalm 15-16

I made it through a week of fasting and I'm content with my accomplishment. It hasn't been easy, but I'm constantly disciplining myself. I believe I'm being led by God to accomplish this task.

It's the first Sunday of the month, so I'm sure my church will have communion. While I get ready for church, I turn on the Turner Broadcasting Network station and listen to Dr. James Merritt preach about why it's easier to be a Christian than not to be. In Matthew 11:29, the Lord says, "Take my yoke upon you and learn from me, for I am gentle and lowly in heart, and you will find rest for your souls." Dr. Merritt explains it is easier to take the yoke of God instead of relying on ourselves. I agree with him. I can say from my own experiences that I did think it was hard to be a Christian. But when I finally began to read my Bible, the Lord spoke to me. He has given me rest in my mind; He has given me rest in my body; He has removed anxiety.

I feel free of my past. Sure, at times I reminisce about past hurts but that is only for a moment. Overall, I am happy and full of life in Jesus Christ. I don't have to rely on myself, because I know from the past that I fail when I do. As I grow closer to God, I want to believe I am becoming more humble. As I grow closer to God, I know I need to rely on Him more and more each day. Each morning, I begin my day with praise and thanks. So far, on this fast, I have not done it wholeheartedly. Listening to Dr. Merritt proves to me that God sends us messages; sometimes they are clear like today and other times, they are just a whisper. However, when we slow down and rest, we can hear God's voice. Thank you, Jesus.

I go home and want to take Top to the dog park. I don't really like the park I've been taking him to, because the dog owners aren't always responsible about their dog's behavior. I go on Yelp and find a new dog park; it's so much closer to home and you can fish there too. Fishing! I have all this free time; I'm going to take up fishing. I haven't fished in years, but I used to be a pretty good fisherman. I caught my first fish with my grandfather in Florida.

My grandfather is a preacher. He baptized me in his pool when I was five years old. He has been my spiritual counselor all of my life and he is the most impactful man in my corner. I respect him immensely. He is a gentleman who has spread the word of God with my grandmother for the past fifty years. When he was younger, he had his own radio show. He was even on *The 700 Club* with Pat Robertson. Now my grandfather is in hospice. Diabetes is taking a toll on him, but he still gives thanks to the Lord, daily. He still loves Jesus no matter what pain he is going through. Every time I think of fishing, I think of my gramps. I'm excited to take up fishing again.

I head to Walmart and purchase a fishing license, a fishing pole, and all the necessities. I go back home and start researching all the public places to fish in Charlotte. Charlotte has a lot of outdoor activities and I'm happy to be in a city that has so much going on. I plan on fishing a couple of times a week. I want to see if I can stock my freezer with fresh bass and trout. Obviously, I can't eat them anytime soon, but I can freeze them for the future.

Once I complete this task I'm going to be more disciplined about the foods I put in my body. I really do want my body to be my temple and I don't think I can do that while eating fast food. So, if I start catching fish, I can filet them and freeze them for the future. It would be pretty cool to have a freezer full of the freshwater fish I caught. I'm going to fish at the local ponds near me first. Then, when I get the hang of it again, I'm going to try out Lake Norman. I really like the Lake Norman area. One of my dreams is to own a lake house. Being around water is calming and soothing to me. I would love to look out from my back porch and see the sunset over the water. I pray the Lord makes me a great fisherman and a great fisher of men.

Day 9

Juice: kale, spinach, apple, organic peanut butter
Bible verses: Proverb 9, Psalm 17–18
Weight: 277.2 lb, 10.3 lb loss

I wake up feeling great today. My pastor's message yesterday, along with Dr. Merritt's words, have given me strength for this journey. I attend University City United Methodist Church in Charlotte. I found this church on Yelp and did my own research.

I remember five years ago, when I was a new believer, going to church by myself was sometimes scary. It takes courage to go to church alone. I don't know why I felt that way, but I fought this fear. I knew I needed the word of God. We took communion at church and I felt the Holy Spirit with me. I felt like I really did have the full armor of God on.

I have my first exam in Ethics today, so I won't be doing any fishing. I need to study and go to school early so I can really concentrate and look over my notes. I feel good about the exam and I'm not worried.

I really like Montreat College and I love my cohort. We've all become close really fast. We share our past hurts and we share how we want to help others who might be facing similar circumstances. It's awesome how God has brought us all together. We all have something to share and something to add. We all come from different walks of life, but we mesh well together. I'm excited to see everyone after spring break and catch up.

We took the midterm exam; it was challenging to say the least.

Day 10

Juice: *kale, spinach, apple, raw honey*
Bible verses: *Proverb 10, Psalm 19-20*

Today, I'm feeling pretty good. I have mental fatigue from my midterm exam, but it's not enough to stop me from having an awesome day. I thought about checking out a modern art museum in South Carolina, but I quickly change my mind to fishing. It's a brisk and sunny morning, and I feel like being out on the lake with my fishing pole. I also had to break the news to my mother that I'm not going to visit for the 4th of July. I just sent her a text without giving her a reason for my absence. I know she won't understand, but I hope she will once I'm finished fasting. Now, my sister texts me back and wants to me to see them on 4th of July. I agree but I don't feel good about it. I think it's important for me to spend the last day of my fast alone, in nature with God—no cell phone, no computer. I really want to spend the hundredth day meditating and reflecting on my accomplishment and journey. I have grown spiritually at an exceptional speed. My grandfather commends me on my spiritual growth all the time. I bet it's hard for my family and people from my past to see the new me or even believe God has transformed me. All I can do is walk it out.

I packed my car with my fishing rod and tackle box. I'm going to fish at Reedy Park and see if I can catch a few fish. I arrive at the park and I don't see anyone at the site. I walk to the trail and find the perfect spot to cast out my line. The sun is shining, the wooded park is quiet, and a brisk wind is blowing. A few minutes go by and I feel a nibble on my line. I didn't catch a fish, but it feels good to be in nature, with God.

The day was a success. I might not have caught any fish, but I had a good time trying. Fishing takes patience. I can hear my dad saying to me, "Did you have fun son?" I answered, "Yea." And my dad said, "Well, that's all that matters." That is so true. I did have a good time fishing. All that really matters is, I tried, I had a good time, and I feel relaxed. I know I'll get the hang of it again once I find the right bait, the right location, and the timing is perfect. Timing is so important in life.

Day  11

Juice: kale, spinach, apple, raw honey
Bible verses: Proverb 11, Psalm 21-22

My emotions are heightened this morning. This is the angriest I've woken up during this fast. My emotions are erratic and my heart is racing. It feels like I'm having an anxiety attack and my heart won't slow down. I don't know where this is coming from. I just woke up, how can I have anxiety? This is one of the issues some veterans deal with. It doesn't happen all the time, but it resurfaces every so often. It creeps up and I can't explain its origins, other than my earlier deployment to Iraq.

I get a hold of myself and settle down enough to take Top to the dog park. It's a beautiful day; the sun is shining and there are a few dogs for Top to play with. I also meet a group of Scottish men who are in a chess club. They ask me if I want to play and I accept the invitation. I haven't played chess in years and I immediately think it's a good way to help focus and channel my emotions. Chess is a game of mental skill; it helps immediately. I am on the defense for most of the game, but the moment quickly switches in my favor once I see a chink in my opponent's armor. My opponent drops his king and I win my first chess match in years.

Today, chess is a metaphor for life. One event in life can make a positive or negative impact. The way I was feeling this morning and how I'm feeling this afternoon have changed drastically. It feels relieving to channel those emotions and I'm happy I was able to do it in a positive way—through chess. I believe God brings people in our life to challenge us, motivate us, love us, and help us grow. Today, the Lord worked through a group of Scottish men who invited me into their chess club.

Day

Juice: kale, spinach, tomato, avocado, green pepper

Bible verses: *Proverb 12, Psalm 23-24*

I wake up calm and immediately look to the wall in my bedroom. I have framed four Bible verses— Ephesians 6:10-18, Psalm 19:4, Psalm 20:6, and Philippians 2:5—that I believe help me focus on the Lord when I first start my day. To me, these four Bible verses are important and I try to live by them daily. I read them aloud and thank the Lord after I've read all four verses. These verses have turned into a daily prayer. I believe it has helped me and I continue to begin my morning with them. I've written down all of the prayer requests in a list for this fast.

So far, the Lord has answered one of the prayers. The prayer is for my mother to find a job closer to her children. The lord has answered this prayer and my mother is moving to Hilton Head, SC. She is happy and excited for the move and my sister and I are excited as well. Our family is also becoming closer, which is another prayer request I wrote for this fast. I believe the Lord relocating my mother will also bring restoration to my family. My parents divorced four years ago and it has been challenging for us all. I believe we are all finally settling into the way life is now.

God has a plan and His grace is sufficient. We are resilient and moving forward, focusing on all the blessings the Lord has brought us.

Today has been a good day. I even went fishing for a bit at Colonel Beatty Park. The fish weren't biting and it was windy. I talked to some of the other fisherman and they weren't getting any bites either. I'm going to keep trying. I change locations to see if I have any better luck catching fish. The fish aren't biting today so I call it quits. Tomorrow is another day. I'll keep trying and hopefully, find the best location to fish.

Tomorrow is the grand opening of the Veterans Affairs Outpatient Clinic in Charlotte. I'm volunteering at the grand opening. There should be a good turn out and I'm excited to network and meet new people.

Day **13**

Juice: *watermelon, banana*
Bible verses: *Proverb 13, Psalm 25-26*

My alarm wakes me up at 5:30 a.m. I lay in bed for about another hour. I'm thinking about today and if I really want to drive to Lake Norman to fish. I finally roll out of bed and decide I'm going to go. I have enough time to fish before I head for the grand opening.

I stop and get gas, and call my dad for some pointers on catching bass. I drive out to the lake; it's beautiful here. It's a bit chilly out, but I'm excited to catch some fish. I go out to the pier and cast my line. I continue the process but so far no luck, not even a bite. The brisk wind is cutting through my fleece and the fish aren't biting again, so I'm calling it a day. I still had a good time exploring Lake Norman.

I feel energetic on my way home. I decide to swim laps at the gym's pool before volunteering at the grand opening of the Veterans Affairs Health Center. The pool is nice and warm—a great escape from Lake Norman's cool breeze. I swim ten laps, but I still have energy. I don't want to overwork my body like I did during the first week of my fast. I can't believe tomorrow is going to be two weeks already. I'm proud of myself for staying consistent. The task still seems daunting, but I'm hoping that, as time progresses, the goal will feel attainable.

The ribbon cutting ceremony is in a few hours and I'm curious to see the newly-built infrastructure. I'm also curious to see who in the community attends the ceremony.

I still feel energetic so far. Today, I woke up early, went fishing, and went to the gym. Now I'm on my way to the ribbon cutting ceremony. I've accomplished a lot already today. I know I'm going to sleep well tonight.

Day 14

Juice: *spinach, watermelon, apple, chia seeds*
Bible verses: *Proverb 14, Psalm 27-28*

It's hard to get out of bed today. I feel physically drained and low on energy. I'm still able to go through my daily rituals of reading my Bible, meditating, and praying. But, other than that, I can tell I won't be moving too fast today.

After I go through my rituals, I lay on the couch watching television. I spend most of the day watching the show *Bizarre Foods* hosted by Andrew Zimmer. I'm on day fourteen of a fast and watching the cooking channel. Cooking relaxes and calms me. I like this show, because the host travels the world trying exotic dishes and foods. I would categorize the show as educational.

I learn a lot laying on my couch today. I feel weary but peaceful.

Cooking is also an art form. The plate is a canvas. I guess that's why I went to culinary school. At one point in my life, I wanted to become a chef. I even worked as a line cook at a restaurant in downtown Austin until I was laid off. It was really a blessing, because I realized I didn't want to be a chef. However, I did learn a lot of great techniques in culinary school, which I still use to this day.

I finally muster the energy to take a shower and take Top to the dog park. There's a dog park really close to my home and Top has a good time romping with the other dogs. After an hour, we're both spent. On the way back home, I decide I'm not going to turn on the television right away. Instead, I'm going to read my Bible for a little bit. I want to meditate on God's word.

I get comfortable in bed and begin reading chapters in Jeremiah, Proverb, and Psalm. The words begin to jump off the page and I want to read more. It finally feels like God is speaking to me! This might sound crazy, but as I read, I can envision future events and I begin to realize where I am in life, the season I'm in, and where I'm heading. God is speaking to me! Words can't describe how I feel right now. I believe when we pray, God hears our voice and when we read our Bible, we hear God's voice. Even though I read my Bible daily, I want to meditate on the word more and more during this fast. I need to hear God's voice every day.

It's funny how this day started and ended. I woke up feeling rundown but mellow. When I began to read my Bible, and really meditate and focus on the words, I began to hear God's voice. Today, I also discovered that the term *Bible* is an acronym: Basic Instructions Before Leaving Earth. It's true—the Bible is a guide and a compass. I want to make sure my internal compass is always pointing toward God.

Today was a good day.

Day **15**

Juice: kale, tomato, zucchini, jalapeño, avocado, black pepper, Italian seasoning
Bible verses: *Proverb 15, Psalm 29-30*

It feels like Groundhog Day. It's hard to get out of bed again. I don't know why I keep feeling like this.

It's day 15 and I'm going to start adding more green vegetables to the juices I make. During the first two weeks, I made juices primarily with fruit. I did this because I knew my body needed more natural sugars in the beginning, since I was purging myself of processed foods, fast foods, and foods that contain a lot of sugar.

During this fast, I mixed kale into almost all my juices, but that's not enough. I need to start adding zucchini, more spinach, green peppers, and celery. When I tell friends and family that zucchini and green peppers— especially green peppers—taste amazing juiced, they cringe. Juiced red peppers taste even better. I also like juicing tomatoes; they taste refreshing and help to hydrate my body. I need to implement carrots sometime, as well.

I've added avocado and jalapeño to my juice today. I only put half of a small jalapeño without the seeds. It gives the juice a great kick. The avocado makes the juice thick and creamy, balancing the bite of the jalapeño.

Around 4:30 p.m., I finally muster up the energy to take Top to the dog park. Top is such a good-natured dog. He plays well with other dogs and everyone at the park loves him. For about an hour, I watch him rollick through the park with the other dogs. Then Top and I finally head back home.

I decide to stop by the gym and swim ten laps. I'm finally starting to feel better, mentally and physically.

I spend the rest of the evening meditating on the word of God.

"A soft answer turns away wrath, but a harsh word stirs up anger."
(Proverb 15:1)

How true it is. I'm trying my best to speak on positive words, even when I'm frustrated with the person I'm conversing with. As I get older, I find myself speaking less. We have a tendency to talk a lot, but say little of value. I want my words to be impactful. I want to speak only when I have something positive, insightful, and impactful to say. It's easier said than done, but that's part of what this fast is all about—purging my body of toxins, physically, spiritually, and metaphorically. I want to feed only my spirit, which will, in turn, nourish my flesh throughout the rest of this fast.

Day 16

Juice: *spinach, zucchini, avocado, jalapeño, tomato*

Bible verses: *Proverb 16, Psalm 31-32*

Weight: 262.4 lb, 23.3 lb loss

I wake up today at 6:30 a.m. and, this time, I feel pretty good. After my morning rituals, I automatically get ready for the gym. I wonder to myself about how I just made this plan to go without worrying about how I might feel after the gym session. I've been cautious long enough about working out during this fast. Working out while on a fast can be dangerous if you push yourself too hard. I've pushed myself in the past to the extent that I became dizzy and even passed out. Shortly after, I wasn't able to continue the fast and fell back into old habits. However, it's time I have faith that I have enough caloric intake to ensure this does not recur.

It's a Monday, so I weigh myself and find I've lost 23.3 pounds! I'm really proud of my discipline and simultaneously, shocked by how much weight I've lost in just fifteen days. I know my lack of energy is due to my recent caloric intake and weight, loss but it has all been worth it. I feel lighter, my mind is fresh, and my thoughts are focused. The aches and pains are still there, but they're not as intense. My body is really changing in a positive way. My body is my temple and it's spring cleaning season in my temple. I truly believe that, with each pound I shed, so are the hurts and hang-ups from my past. My clothes fit more snugly and now those outfits I packed away fit too. I'm really happy with the immense changes I have made.

The key is to trust God and take it one day at a time—don't look too far into the future. I'm going to treat this fast like a football game. There are four quarters in a football game and each twenty-five days is another quarter complete. There is light at the end of the tunnel and I imagine how I'm going to look on day 100. All I need to do is take things gradually and keep feeding my spirit through God's word.

Day 17

Juice: spinach, zucchini, banana, apple, watermelon, aloe, organic peanut butter
Bible verses: *Proverb 17, Psalm 33-34*

I have clarity this morning and I'm immediately conscience of it. I'm alert, I feel good, and I'm not fatigued. However, I have zero motivation to leave my apartment today. I just want to watch movies and relax. During this season of rest, I haven't really rested. I quit my job in January. It has been three months and I still wake up at sunrise as if I have something to do—that something is learning to rest. So, today, I'm actually content with watching movies all day.

I want to make a different kind of juice today. I have an aloe plant, which is growing quite nicely, but a couple of the leaves are breaking off, so I'm going to juice them. I know it probably sounds weird, but you can actually eat or juice aloe leaves. The inside of the aloe leaf is edible; it's known as the aloe latex. I sharpen my chef's knife and delicately slice the outer leaf off. I'm surprised by how much latex was in that one leaf. I add it to my blender, with all the other fruits and vegetables, and juice it. Based on the research I've done, aloe is supposed to be good for the immune system and it's a natural detoxifier. I can't taste it but it's cool to know I'm trying something new.

While reading *Psalm 33*, a verse immediately makes itself prominent to me:

> *"No king is saved by the size of his army;*
> *no warrior escapes by his great strength."*
> *(Psalm 33:16)*

When I was honorably discharged from the army, I felt like I was invincible for surviving two tours to Iraq. It was a false sense of invincibility, because at home, I was self-treating myself with alcohol, marijuana, and sex. However, when I went out into the world, I felt like I couldn't be killed. It scares me when I look back on these times, because now I realize the many times I put myself in harm's way and didn't care.

Life is challenging sometimes, especially when you're alone. I know I was self-medicating because when I finally sat down and tried to relax, I missed being a part of something bigger than myself. I missed the army, but I felt burned out by it. So many veterans can relate to this feeling.

The challenge is to find purpose. I think this is what all of mankind is searching for. What is my purpose? I'm still trying to figure my own life out, but I do know part of my purpose is to help others.

Day 18

Juice: spinach, tomato, avocado, zucchini, green pepper
Bible verses: Proverb 19, Psalm 35-36

Today was a good day.

This morning I took Top to the dog park so I could meet with my Scottish friends for chess. I ended up losing both the games I played. I had a good chance of winning the second match, but I became inpatient during a move and, as a result, my queen was killed. I immediately saw my mistake and knew my impatience would lead to my defeat. What a great metaphor for life: timing is everything and I'm learning the importance of patience through this fast, fishing, and now chess. One wrong decision can make a huge difference.

I really like reading the book of Psalms in the Bible, because much of the book details David and his words. I can relate to King David of Israel in so many ways. David is a man after God's own heart. He had to fight for everything in his life and his experiences consist of extreme highs and lows.

David is a great warrior and kills the giant, Goliath. He is then anointed to be the next king of Israel and he marries into royalty. David proves himself a great leader, but his lows are extreme. One day, David sees Bathsheba, the wife of Uriah (one of David's military officers), bathing on the roof and he becomes intrigued with her. David commits adultery with Bathsheba and she becomes pregnant. He sends Uriah into battle and Uriah is killed.

The story of David is intriguing. It shows the impact of decision-making, good or bad, and how it determines the journey our life will take. The decisions we make affect all of the people in our lives. This fast, however, is helping me gain better control over my impulses, so I can make wise decisions.

Day **19**

Juice: spinach, tomato, avocado, jalapeño, cayenne pepper, green pepper

Bible verses: Proverb 19, Psalm 37-38

Top has a big day today. He's meeting his new dog sitter, who will watch him when I'm away on weekend trips. The sitter will come home and let him out, watching over him all the while. This is going to require a lot of trust on my part.

I bought Top from a breeder when he was ten weeks old and we've been almost inseparable ever since. But I'm traveling to Atlanta, Georgia (GA) next week to see my uncle and take him to an Atlanta Braves game. One of the reasons I moved back to the east coast was so I could see my family more often. I haven't seen my uncle in years. Now that I live in Charlotte, he is only four hours away. I'm excited to see him and check out a baseball stadium I haven't been to before.

The Braves are playing my favorite team, the New York Mets. I've been a Mets fan for as long as I can remember. The 1986 Mets are the best Mets team and my baseball hero growing up was Darryl Strawberry. He was exciting to watch. It's ironic that my favorite baseball player also had a terrible addiction to cocaine and self-medication.

One day, I was watching the Christian television station, Trinity Broadcasting Network (TBN), and I was shocked to see Darryl Strawberry preaching the word of God. Through God, Strawberry changed himself and committed his life to Jesus Christ. He and his wife also opened the Darryl Strawberry Recovery Center in Florida. I was glued to the television throughout the episode. His actions moved me to tears and I couldn't admire my childhood more. I was in the beginning stages of my graduate program in Clinical Mental Health Counseling at the time. Back then, I focused on how the people in my life were going to judge me as unqualified to be a therapist, rather than on how God has called me to serve. In so many ways, I wanted validation that I was on the right track.

When we open our eyes and become still, God will show us His path. More often than not, it will be subtle and we'll have to pay particular attention to our relationship with God to hear His message. God sent me a sign through my childhood hero that I didn't need validation from anyone. The best aspect about God is he can use anyone to convey His message, and He often uses people who nobody believes in. The best example of this is Jesus's disciples. They were fishermen, tax collectors, and common men.

We'll all make mistakes in life, but no matter the size of the mistake, God can use us. I thought of that moment when I saw Darryl Strawberry on television today, because I'm confident that I'm on the right path now. I'm no longer on a selfish path to further my own good; I'm on a path to further the common good by listening to God and how he wants me to serve.

I feel good today, especially about my future. I believe that when we have peace in our life, it is God's way of letting us know we are on the right path.

Day 20

Juice: banana, watermelon, chia seeds, raw honey, organic peanut butter
Bible verses: Proverb 21, Psalm 39-40

This is the best juice I've ever tasted! Seriously, I was overcome with happiness as soon as I had the first sip. The peanut butter makes it silky smooth; the watermelon makes the juice refreshing; the chia seeds add thickness; the raw honey is a natural sweetener, and banana juice is my favorite.

A juice like this brings the wind to my sails on this fast. I really needed this today, because I've been thinking about the foods I really miss. I've also realized how long it's going to be until I eat. I'm taking it one day at a time, but I don't think it helps that most of the shows I've recorded are cooking shows. I'm subconsciously torturing myself and now it's becoming a problem. Writing this out helps me realize I need to stop recording cooking shows immediately.

It's Friday and I take Top to the dog park this morning, so I can meet with my chess club mates. When I get there, I find they are already focused on a match. I hope to get at least one win today. I end up against the best chess player in the group, Andy, and he slaughters me in about five minutes. The great thing about him is, even though he slaughters me, he's still humble. He's willing to go out of his way and teach me some crucial moves and how to counter my opponent's next move. I lost all the chess matches today, but I had a great time with the guys.

This fast is helping me grow to perceive my emotional triggers and what can hold me back.

Day 21

Juice: *spinach, zucchini, avocado, jalapeño, green pepper*

Bible verses: *Proverb 22, Psalm 41-42*

The sun is shining and the weather is amazing today. I woke up this morning with one thing on my mind: I will not procrastinate on my papers and projects. I have an Ethics paper due on Monday and I usually wait twenty-four hours before writing my papers. I procrastinate on purpose; the pressure helps me focus on the assignment. This isn't a new concept to me; I've been writing papers under this model ever since I began earning my bachelor's degree. No matter how large the paper or project, I wait for forty-eight to twenty-four hours before I sit down to begin working on it. However, I research and formulate the concept in my head, thinking about it all week. I no longer want to operate this way. Instead, I want to discipline myself to be responsible.

It might sound corny, but I looked up quotes and positive memes on procrastination. I found two that inspire me. The first quote is from Chuck Swindoll, an evangelical pastor, author, and educator.

"The habit of always putting off an experience until you can afford it, or until the time is right, or until you know how to do it is one of the greatest burglars of joy. Be deliberate, but once you've made up your mind—jump in."

This quote really speaks to me, because when I have something I need to complete, all I do is think about it. So, instead of beginning it, I wait until the last minute to work on it. The second quote is by successful inspirational author, Jacob Reimer, from his work, *Rich Habits – 33 Daily Habits of the Rich & Wealthy!*

"You, as a person who wants to be successful, need to make 'I'm doing it now' a part of your daily vocabulary. Not, 'I'll do it after this email,' or 'I'll do it tonight.'"

This quote is so true. We can accomplish so many things in our life today, but instead, we put it off until tomorrow. This is another reason I'm doing this fast. I saw myself putting on weight, but instead of doing something about it right away, I kept putting it off. Looking back on it now, I really lacked discipline when it came to my diet. Working in sales and sitting at a desk are easy excuses for all of us to make when we let go of our discipline toward health.

I decided today that I will no longer procrastinate about anything I do. I began working on my case study for Ethics and I made up my mind that I'd complete it today. I want to discipline myself to research, write, and formulate this case study. Once I completed my research, the words came to me and I began to write. I took a few breaks in between, but I completed it and submitted the assignment by early afternoon. Instead of being under pressure to complete it, I now have peace for completing it.

I'm so happy right now. I want to remember this feeling, so that, when the next assignment arrives, I can remind myself of this moment and continue to be diligent.

Day 22

Juice: spinach, apple, organic zucchini, raw honey

Bible verses: Proverb 22, Psalm 43-44

After completing my Ethics assignment yesterday, I went to the dog park and then went fishing. While fishing, I began having back spasms and I could barely walk. A back injury from Iraq has become a constant problem in my life. I have back spasms that come and go and lately, they seem to be staying a lot longer.

My back hurts so bad right now, I can barely bend over. I lie on the couch and decide I'm not going to church today. Instead, I watch preachers on television and lay as flat as I can on my back. Pastor Jentezen Franklin's program comes on and I'm inspired to try and make it to church.

I take an extra-long shower and try to stretch my back, but I'm as stiff as a board. Each step I take hurts and I can barely bend down to tie my shoes, but I'm adamant to not let my pain get in the way. I make it to church successfully, but I can barely concentrate on the pastor's message. All my focus is on the pain.

Mentally, I feel great. My reflection in the full-length mirror shows me how much weight I've lost. I feel healthy and I'm proud of how this drastic change is going to have lasting benefits. However, this irritating back pain is unbearable. I go to the gym and sit in the whirlpool to try and loosen up my back muscles. I sit up against the jets for about an hour. The muscles in my back feel like they're loosening up, but the pain is annoying.

I spend the rest of the day lying down on the couch, to rest my back. I think it's time I finally see a chiropractor and see if a permanent solution to my injury can be determined.

Even though I'm in pain, I feel good mentally and I will not let the pain take away my joy. Laying here on the couch, I keep repeating to myself, "Don't let the pain overcome the joy."

Day **23**

Juice: avocado, celery, green pepper, green onion, jalpeño, carrot
Bible verses: Proverb 23, Psalm 45-46
Weight: 258.3 lb, 29.2 lb loss

I've now lost 29.2 pounds in twenty-three days. This has been an emotional rollercoaster—feeling dizzy and bedridden from fatigue at times—but days like today make it all worth it. My mind is clear and I have a laser-like focus. I feel light and my clothes are beginning to feel really loose. Moments like this make me realize how great I'm going to feel on day 100.

I'm adamant about seeing a chiropractor. I call and make an appointment, happy to hear I can visit this morning. I arrive at the clinic, fill out the required documents, and now I'm off to see if the doctor can help my back. He realigns my back and I can feel the stress has left my body. He informs me it's more of a muscle issue than bone or nerve damage, which is really good to hear. Today has started off really well.

Since I feel well and my body feels relaxed, I might as well run some errands. I need to go to the grocery store. Since day 25 is in two days, I've made up my mind that I'm going to begin juicing more vegetables and less fruit. I want to focus on green vegetables, since I get the most energy from green juices. While in the produce section, I pick up fresh spinach, avocados, green onions, tomatoes, bananas, carrots, jalapeños, green peppers, and celery.

I'm going to put half an avocado in each juice. I really like the rich and creamy flavor of avocados. I'm also going to do something different and add green onion to the mix.

I love green onions. I also love making sandwiches. When I make sandwiches, I don't just use mayonnaise; I make an aioli and always add green onion to the aioli. I like juices to have a bit of bite to them, so I'm going to try juicing a green onion. Back in culinary school, I learned in nutrition class, that it's a good rule to eat as wide a variety of colored fruits and vegetables as possible. I agree with this rule. The only fruits I have are apples and bananas. I didn't have too many apples last week, but this week moving forward, I will juice apple and bananas as a treat to add more natural sugar to my diet. I really like the juice I made today with the wide range of vegetables. This is going to be my staple juice for a week or so.

Day 24

Juice: *avocado, green pepper, green onion, spinach, carrot, celery, and jalapeño*
Bible verses: Proverb 24, Psalm 46 –47

"If you faint in the day of adversity, Your strength is small."
(Proverb 24:10)

This verse stood out to me, while I was reading the Bible. I love how the Bible makes the reader confront who they truly are. Not everyone has a person in their life who will be honest enough with them to let them know if they are on the right track or not.

Today, I feel strong, but lately, I've been resentful toward my family. A lot of anger has been stirring up within me. After reading this verse, however, I know I need to be strong, let go of past hurts, and look to God for healing. The enemy can't attack me with drugs, alcohol, or women anymore, so now the enemy is trying old tricks. I need to realize God is with me; God is sovereign and He has given me the authority to stand up to the enemy and fight. I have the full armor of God today.

I'm pretty excited about this evening. I'm going to my first Charlotte Knights baseball game. They are playing the Norfolk Tides. But to me, the coolest part of the game is my childhood baseball hero, Darryl Strawberry, who will be there signing autographs. Life is funny sometimes; just the other day, I was watching him on TBN and now he's going to be in the "Queen's City" to sign autographs.

I get to the stadium and a queue has formed outside of the gate. I brought my 1988 Topps All-Star Daryl Strawberry baseball card. The card is from his early days and when I was a Mets fanatic.

It's finally my turn to meet Strawberry. I say to him, "Nice to meet you, Mr. Strawberry, thank you for sharing your testimony on TBN." He says in his deep voice, "Oh yeah." I inform him that I'm a graduate student studying clinical mental health counseling and I've read all about Strawberry Ministries and the counseling center he has built to help those in need. He shakes my hand, seemingly impressed, and gives me a wink. At this point, I'm pretty happy to say the least. I just met my childhood baseball hero.

He is interviewed and the sports reporter asks him about his relationship with baseball Hall of Famer and Met catcher Gary Carter. He tells the audience that Gary Carter was a man of God and, even though they were playing at the highest level of baseball, he did not let the temptations thrown at him derail his walk with Christ. Strawberry says he was always impressed with Carter's Christian faith. It's awesome to hear people share their intimate moments about how God made an impression on their lives through other people.

In twenty-four hours, I'll have made it through the first quarter of this fast. I feel great and I'm excited about tomorrow.

Day 25

Juice: *spinach, avocado, green pepper, green onion, celery, carrot, jalapeño*
Bible verses: *Proverb 25, Psalm 48-49*
First Quarter weigh in: *257.0 lb, 30.5 lb loss*

The first quarter of my fast is over! Looking back to day 1, I know I had some challenging days, but overall, the majority of this fast has helped me learn about who I am. I'm gradually becoming conscious of my thoughts and feelings. I've completed the first step in purging my body of toxicities. It feels good to hit this milestone, but I still have a long way to go.

Now that I've completed the first quarter, I've decided to make juices that have more of a vegetable base rather than fruits. For the past couple of days that I've done this, I notice I have a lot more energy and I'm thinking more clearly. My skin looks great and my Ethics professor even commented that I look different. I notice the weight loss mostly in my face and in how my clothes feel.

Not only is it day 25 but it's also time for my art therapy class for veterans. I love this class. I've been thinking all week about what I'm going to paint. I hope it looks as good on canvas as it does in my mind. I arrive at the Matthews Arts Center, greet everyone, and then I begin to set up and paint. I begin painting what I had initially thought of, but I decide it no longer matches how I feel. Instead, I paint an abstract painting, which matches my mood and the colors I feel. I use a lot of purple, white, red, and mix a few colors to come up with a soothing tone. I'm really proud of how this painting has turned out.

I have a lot of energy today and I'm attacking the next twenty-five days with hope and positive vibrations. I can only thank God for the progress I've made on my journey and how good I feel about myself. I know God is with me and He will bless me throughout this fast. I don't know what the next twenty-five days will bring, but so far, I'm really thankful for how this fast has challenged me and how I've learned so much about my thoughts and emotions.

Day 26

Juice: avocado, green pepper, green onion, jalapeño, carrot

Bible verses: Proverb 26, Psalm 50-51

I had the urge to clean today–to clean everything. It began with making an appointment at the dog groomer's. I dropped Top off. His coat looks rough and he needs a trim. He seems to be shedding a good deal lately and, being the clean freak that I am, there's too much dog hair everywhere for me to tolerate. I then go home and bug bomb my apartment, take my laundry with me, put it in the trunk of my car, and head off to the self-service car wash. I want to vacuum my car and clean the interior.

After the wash, I continue my journey to Uptown. I have a group project I need to work on and I'm going to assemble the project at Amelie's French Bakery & Cafe. This will also allow me the opportunity to air out my apartment for the next couple of hours.

After working on the project for a couple of hours, I stop by Montreat to speak to my advisor, Mary. The subject of dynamics in relationships comes up and she shares with me Mark 6:4.

"A prophet is not without honor except in his own country, among his own relatives, and in his own house."

These words, which Jesus spoke, hit me like a ton of bricks. The dynamics of my past relationships haven't changed, even though I've matured and grown as a man. Mary explained to me that Jesus might have me alone for this season, so I can grow in him and build a strong relationship with him. I agree and everything is beginning to make sense.

I grew up in Lancaster, Pennsylvania, in a melting pot of so many different types of people. It was a good place to grow up and I can't complain about my education or the community. I like the people and the strong Pennsylvania Dutch culture. However, I've had an issue with visiting the place since I left many years ago. I was a wild child who behaved immaturely. I might have had a good heart, but I was a bully at times, sometimes ignorant or hurtful. I didn't care about how I carried myself or what people thought of me. I lived for myself and myself only.

Now, a grown man, I'm much different. I don't know who my past self is anymore, but when I go home, everyone is sure to remind me. The hypocrisy of the situation is everyone who was my friend, was right there with me during the drinking, drugs, and ignorant moments. They want to make sure everyone forgets who they used to be and, instead, be respected for who they are today. Everything in my life, good and bad, has always been magnified. I don't know why. When I heard Mary speaking Jesus's words, it all made sense.

I went home and started my laundry. While waiting for Top to be finished at the groomer's and my clothes to finish, I read Mark 6:4 over and over. I meditated on Jesus's words and they lingered on my tongue.

I decided to take a drastic step and change my phone number. I've had the same number for over ten years. A lot of women, drug dealers, and friends from my past have that number. It's time to break away from who that number represents. I feel liberated.

Looking back on the day's accomplishments, I did a lot of cleaning. This is exactly what I need right now. This day is replete with peace and I feel cleansed. It feels good to control who should be in my life now—to know those who are, are the ones I want in my life.

Jesus's words will stand out to us when we take the time to meditate and read the Bible. Day 26 has been a great start to the next quarter of this fast. Thank you, Jesus, and thank you for answering my prayers today. When I prayed today, I cried, asking the Lord to encourage me. He brought me His word by using my advisor to share it with me and plant that seed. When I was leaving Amelie's I was going to go straight to the parking garage and then go home, but something told me to stop by Montreat and say hi to Mary. That something was God. It's amazing how one little change in our direction can be impactful.

Day 27

Juice: *kale, spinach, celery, jalapeño, green pepper*
Bible verses: *Proverb 27, Psalm 52-53*

One more day before I travel to Atlanta to see my uncle and his family and go to the Braves game. They're playing my team, the Mets. I'm excited to visit a new baseball stadium. I've never been to Atlanta either; I've only driven through it. I learn a lot from different cultures and cities so I can't wait to see the culture of Atlanta.

I discovered something important during the Charlotte Knights game: it's really hard to fast while attending a baseball game. That was the first time I didn't eat a hotdog at baseball game. My curiosity got the best of me; it was a new stadium and I wanted to see the game from all angles, so I left my seat and began to walk around. I began to smell hotdogs, barbecue, and pretzels. All the smells were really messing with my mind. I ended up leaving in the middle of the third inning, because the smells were so intense. I can only imagine the memories the smells will bring me when I visit Turner Field tomorrow night.

Through this fast and breaking away from the world, I'm learning to control my impulses, as well as my focus. And tomorrow will be a great test of this; I must not let my mind wander. To focus my mind, I will concentrate on the game, the players, and having good conversations with my uncle. Each time a smell triggers my brain, I'll immediately use my phone to look up the baseball player who is up to bat or ask my uncle a question. I'm going to master the art of focus and the art of being calm. The smells trigger anxiety and anxiety triggers nervousness. I've noticed all of my professors possess a calm energy. I want to possess this as well. I asked my Ethics professor how a counselor in training exemplifies calm. "Through your maturity in this program and with your experiences as a counselor, you will master the art of calm," she replied. The phrase, "master of calm," impressed itself upon my mind. One person, in my opinion, who is a master of calm, is President Barack Obama. No matter what a person's political view is, it's hard to argue that he hasn't mastered the art of being calm.

Throughout all of the ridicule, I've never seen him become flustered or lose his cool. It must take discipline, focus, and practice not to react how the flesh wants to react but to think logically. I have struggled in this regard. I mean, I've grown a lot, but I'll always encounter people who push my buttons too far. However, not reacting and keeping cool and calm will say volumes about my maturity.

Day 28

Juice: banana, apple, carrot, raw honey, organic peanut butter

Bible verses: Proverb 28, Psalm 54-55

I said "bye" to Top and began my road trip to Atlanta. Google Maps informed me my trip was only three and a half hours from my uncle's. I didn't realize I was that close to him. When I get on the road, I have a few hours to drive and think.

I feel great. I have a lot of energy and I'm excited to see Turner Field and watch the Mets beat the Braves. I've been thinking how long it has been since I've seen my Uncle David. I really don't even remember; I just know I always have a great time with him. He is a cool guy with a big heart. He has always been a soft-spoken, intelligent, and kind man. He is also business savvy; when I do see him, he's always in my ear giving me financial advice.

I finally arrive at his office and greet him warmly. He takes me around and introduces me to his employees, and we talk for a bit before he gets back to work. I take a nap in my car to waste time before we head to the game. When he's finally done with work, we drive to his place in the suburbs of Atlanta—not too far from the game. We finally get close enough and I see the stadium. I'm eager to park and get to our seats.

I begin to feel the energy of the crowd as we walk into Turner Field. We walk around and find our section, walk down to our seat, and take a look at the field. We have great seats, fifteen rows from first base. The game is exciting and the fans around us are a mixture of Mets and Braves, but everyone is friendly. I had a lot of time to hang out with my uncle and talk and laugh. The time we spent together was amazing; we had a good deal of time to catch up.

We leave at the top of the eighth inning to beat the traffic. My uncle drives me around to show me Atlanta. We drive down Peachtree St. and he shows me the Fox Theatre; then he takes me on a tour through the downtown area. I begin to really fall in love with Atlanta. The people are really friendly and there's a lot to do. I can feel the energy I haven't felt since I left Austin. I could really see myself living here one day. We get back to his house and I get to hang out with my cousin Devon for a little bit before going to bed.

I needed this day. It was a time to fill up on love, wisdom, joy, and encouragement. I'm so glad I came to visit my uncle.

Day 29

Juice: banana, apple, carrot, raw honey, organic peanut butter

Bible verses: Proverb 29, Psalm 56-57

The next morning, I'm greeted by a big smile and hug from my aunt Gloria. We all sit, talk, and share laughs together before I leave for Charlotte.

I learn a lot about my family. My uncle tells me stories of his childhood, my grandmother, who passed away two years before I was born, and my mother. One of the stories about my grandmother really touched me. On the whole, all of the stories my uncle shared softened my heart and gave me insight and understanding. While he shared all of this with me, I thought about why I really came: I wanted to learn about my family—to learn about me.

I say goodbye to my family and I start my trip back to Charlotte. I think about the stories my uncle shared and envision what my family has been through. We have all been through a lot, but we are resilient and happy. I believe life's challenges have brought our family closer. I'm happy to be close to my uncle and know I can visit him anytime. It feels good to be around family again. It has been nearly fifteen years since I've lived around my family. When I joined the army, I was first stationed in Germany for three years. I re-enlisted and picked Fort Hood, TX as my next duty station. After less than sixty days of my boots hitting Texas soil, I was in Iraq for my first tour. After my tour, I was back in Texas for eleven months, and then back to Iraq for my second tour, which lasted fifteen months. The second tour was the closest I've been to letting life's challenges break me. I went through a lot during that period, and even though I wasn't practicing my faith wholeheartedly, I still prayed and maintained a relationship with God when it was convenient for me. My uncle, Ray, passed away while I was in Iraq. He was the comedian out of all my uncles. I was really upset about his death, and especially because I was unable to attend his funeral. I had relationship issues with a girl back in Texas. I was stressed about my relationship with my fellow soldiers and leaders. The online college course I took up was causing me additional strain. I became extremely weary and depressed. However, I made it through and I'm still standing and smiling. I needed those life challenges. I needed them, because they brought me closer to God. If it wasn't for life's struggles, my relationship with God might have never grown. When people ask me, "What was Iraq like?" I always answer with "humbling." In 2016, there are people on this planet who do not get clean water—a basic necessity for humans to survive. I always think about that: someone in the world is searching for clean water right now. In comparison to this, my struggles were miniscule. I thank God for my struggles.

Day 30

Juice: *green, orange, and red pepper, green onion, jalapeño, tomato, radish, avocado*
Bible verses: *Proverb 30, Psalm 58-59*
Workout: *back extension, chest press, lat pull-down, row/rear deltoid, shoulder press, high row, triceps, incline press, biceps*
Weight: *251 lb, 36.5 lb loss*

It's day 30 and I feel great! I just realized I've been consistently fasting for *thirty* days. I feel a lot stronger and more energized since changing my juice recipes to a vegetable base. I've now lost 36.5 pounds and I notice the weight loss in my face and midsection. Clothes I had stored away now fit and my attitude is a lot happier. I've been in a really good mood and I notice I have a smile on my face without any apparent cause. I'm going to celebrate my successful thirty-day fast with a workout at the YMCA.

My plan is to use the elliptical machines and do one set of as many repetitions as possible before moving on to another machine. The reason I'm only working my upper body, is because my lower body is already solid. I was born with a naturally strong lower body—my calves and quads are firm. Now, I want to strengthen my back, midsection, and chest. These are my problem areas and I want to attack the areas that are weak.

I had a good workout and it gave me more energy. I'm going to do this workout three to four times a week. Since I'm losing weight so fast, I'm concerned about losing muscle as well; so, I want to combat my weight loss with weight lifting.

I feel strong today. I'm motivated to make more drastic changes while on this fast. I'm making everlasting changes for me and my family.

Today was an amazing day. All praise goes to God.

Day 31

Juice: *green, red, and yellow pepper, kale, avocado, spinach, jalapeño, green onion, carrot, tomato, celery*
Bible verses: *Proverb 31, Psalm 60-61*

Since I've been in graduate school, I like to use Tuesday as a personal day. On this day, I usually go to the museum, see a movie, explore something new, or just relax at home.

Today, I've decided to go to the movie theater and see *Miracles from Heaven*; it's based on a true story about a family in Texas. The theme of the story is faith—having faith in God's miraculous power while facing the challenging moments in our life. Jennifer Garner plays the mother of a daughter who is dying of a rare condition. To avoid giving the plot away, I'll just say that the little girl is healed.

The faith-based movie spoke to me about the different areas of my faith. It also showed me how much I've grown in my walk. I empathized with Garner's role. When we are challenged and begin to lose faith, that is when we are being tested. When God does not show up when we expect Him to, we become frustrated and resentful. Not only have I cried out to God but I've also cursed Him, blasphemed Him, and said the worst things I could never repeat again. I've been so angry with God that I didn't understand why I was still alive and why He didn't just let me die in Iraq.

To me, being powerless is the worst feeling. I believe it is the worst type of hurt, because you can't do anything about it. Our faith is repeatedly tested to help us grow in the image God made us. It isn't easy but, when I look back at several of the tests God has put me through, I understand why He made me go through it all. He strips us to equip us. Now, I laugh at a lot of the same things that hurt me in the past. When people make snide or hurtful comments about me, I laugh it off. God taught me to pity those people for their ignorance. He also taught me to pray for them regardless. There was a time when I would pray God would kill certain people and, not just kill them but make it a painful, torturous death. Those types of prayers don't help anyone; it might feed the desire of my flesh for a minute, but I know it's wrong. Now, I pray for the healing of that person. I might not be so forgiving in the heat of the moment, but once I calm down, I let it go and leave it to God, reciting a quick prayer of healing for that person.

Day 32

Juice: *green, yellow, red pepper, avocado, tomato, celery, kale, spinach, jalapeño*
Bible verses: *Matt1-2, Psalm 62-63*
Workout: *lat pulldown, chest press, mid row, pec fly, shoulder press, bicep, seated dip, low back, leg press, triceps*

I woke up this morning with a lot of energy. I'm laughing and I'm in a great mood. I'm so excited to expect a miracle today.

My day is filled with tasks I need to complete. I first go to the gym and get a solid workout. My routine is moving from machine to machine, medium to lightweight, doing two sets of ten repetitions. I began the workout only doing one set, but I felt so good I decided to add another set. It's important to listen to your body and today, my body wants to lift weights. I'm not light-headed at all and after my shower, I feel amazing. I love the feeling of showering after a workout most: I feel refreshed, calm, and it puts me in a good mood.

I'm off to finish my last case study for Ethics. Amelie's Bakery is my new hangout and that's where I go to write my case study. Once again, I'm a procrastination killer, attacking full force. The words are flowing and I complete my case study five days before the assignment is due.

My mind is clear and alert. I love how juiced vegetables promote clarity and positive emotions. I do a mental assessment of how I used to feel when I was killing myself with an improper diet earlier. I'm learning to assess my feelings while drinking my juice to see how it affects my brain function.

Today, I began reading the book of Matthew. The subject of this book is Jesus and it presents Him as the King of the Jews, the Messiah. The book of Matthew explains Jesus's genealogy, baptism, messages, and miracles. Matthew explains why Christ is King. Another goal I'm setting is to read the four Gospels of the New Testament—Matthew, Mark, Luke, and John—before this fast is over. The four Gospels explain who Jesus is.

Even though I give a lot of attention to how my fast is making me feel. I want to make sure I'm fasting for the right reasons: to become closer to God and learn about Jesus.

Day 33

Juice: green, red, and orange peppers, avocado, spinach, kale, tomato, celery, green onion, radish

Bible verses: Matt 3-4, Psalm 64-65

My body is feels the previous workouts and I am exhausted this morning. I feel lazy and I am emotionally and physically tired. I don't think I am going to do much of anything today. I go through my daily rituals and make a juice but I barely drink any. I want to lie in bed and watch movies and be lazy. I might have been pushing myself too hard but I have loved every moment of it. I love going to the gym and having a daily routine centered on health.

I am happy with the progress I have made but I need to rest today. I spend the day watching movies and sleeping. I took a nap in the morning and a nap in the afternoon. I didn't realize how much rest I needed. I have been learning how important rest and sleep is to the body. When I was in the Army for eight years I didn't sleep much. I was always driving on missions throughout Germany and working hard and playing hard. That seems to be the military way: "work hard play hard." When I was stationed in Germany I would go out five days a week. That was after physical training and working. I had a weekly routine of which bars and clubs I would go to. Many mornings I was drunk in formation and was reprimanded to the point I was told if I showed up drunk to formation I was going to be demoted. I don't reminisce much but when I do I am always shocked at the reckless lifestyle I lived. It always makes me realize God has a strong hand on me.

Day 34

Juice: *green, red, and orange peppers, avocado, spinach, kale, tomato, celery, green onion, radish*
Bible verses: *Matt 5-6, Psalm 66-67*
Workout: *back extension, chest press, lat pulldown, row/rear deltoid, shoulder press, high row, triceps, incline press, biceps*

My workout today was incredible. I'm becoming stronger and I can see the definition in my chest, shoulders, and arms. Ever since I began fasting and consuming a large quantity of vegetables, I have focus during my workout, which I never had before. In the past, my anxiety could cause me to rush through my workouts. I wanted to exercise, but I wanted it to finish as soon as I began. Now, I focus on the muscle group I'm building and envision the muscle growing while burning fat.

Pumping Iron, the bodybuilding documentary centered on Arnold Schwarzenegger and Lou Ferrigno, is a must-watch for anyone interested in bodybuilding. Schwarzenegger explains how he focuses during muscle building. Watching the documentary and listening to Arnold speak, you realize how he came to be the specimen of a man he is. I think about what he says sometimes when I'm working out. I want to have that kind of focus in everything I do in life.

Later today, I received a call from my dad. I was surprised to see his name appear on my phone, because he never calls. I knew it must be important. My grandfather has been in hospice for about a month. My dad informed me that my grandfather's health has become worse and I could tell it was serious by the careful manner in which he spoke. He told me that he would keep me up-to-date on my grandfather's health. After speaking with him, I called my grandmother. She sounded exhausted and overwhelmed. I asked her if Grandpa had enough strength to speak with me. I could hear her talking to him and he sounded disoriented. She handed him the phone and I spoke with him briefly. I told him Isaiah 6:8 spoke to me today and I told him to "let go and let God." He repeated what I said and

I told him I love him. I thanked him for always being a man in my corner, an encourager, and a loving man. He told me he loved me too and hung up.

I felt the weight of the world on my shoulders and I immediately felt emotionally spent. I was so tired I had to lie down. I just laid there and wondered if that was the last time I would ever hear from my grandfather. I prayed and opened my Bible to Psalm 23:

> *The Lord is my shepherd; I shall not want. He maketh me lie down in green pastures: he leadeth me beside the still waters. He restoreth my soul; he leadeth me in the paths of righteousness for his name's sake. Yea, though I walk through the valley of the shadow of death, I will fear no evil; for thou art with me; thy rod and thy staff they comfort me. Thou preparest a table before me in the presence of mine enemies: thou anointest my head with oil; my cup runneth over. Surely goodness and mercy shall follow me all the days of my life: and I will dwell in the house of the Lord forever.*

I felt a sense of peace come over me, but I still felt worn out. I don't want my grandfather to suffer any more and I kept asking God to "bring him home." It's selfish of me to want him to live just so I can have him around. I'd rather he be in heaven, healed and at peace. I see peace in death, because I know I will be with God. My grandfather has always told he wants people to rejoice at his funeral. He doesn't want them to be sad. He wants them to be happy that he is "home" with Jesus. Remember, my grandfather is the person who introduced me to God and baptized me at his pool when I was six years old. My grandmother was there as well. It was just the three of us and my grandparents perfectly explained who Jesus is and what baptism is. At six years old, I fully understood what they said. I'm blessed to have such great grandparents, who have taught me a lifetime of wisdom. Introducing me to Jesus and sharing His wisdom is the best gift I've received from my grandfather. I have been praying the Lord favors my grandmother with peace and strength for these end times. I'm also praying that my grandfather's death isn't going to be an excuse for my dad, uncle, brothers, and sisters to drink excessively and fall into depression. Instead, I am hoping they come together for my grandmother and for each other.

I prepare for his death by meditating on God's word, being silent, and listening to God. The thought of having a drink or smoking marijuana crosses my mind and I catch myself. I quickly fight it off, but learn something important. Death breeds temptation. Death is a perfect time for the enemy to creep up and put negative thoughts into our head. Life is more about spiritual warfare then anyone believes. Sometimes, the enemy is blatant, but most of the time he's subtle. Anyone who's adamant about living a righteous lifestyle must be aware of the spiritual battle going on in our minds and body. This fast is providing me with so much clarity, I can see the enemy creeping from a mile away.

Today I feel strong even though I am fatigued. My flesh might feel weak but my spirit is strong because God is with me.

Day 35

Juice: green pepper, spinach, kale, tomato, avocado, celery, carrot

Bible verses: Matt 7-8, Psalm 68-69

This morning, I called my grandparents' house to check on my grandfather and my dad answered. The fact that he was at their house so early in the morning, added to the severity of my grandfather's health condition, cause me great worry. I spoke with him and he told me my grandfather is getting worse. He told me he would let me know if anything changed and we hung up. After talking to my dad, I went to the grocery store to stock up on vegetables. On the way there, I thought about driving to Pennsylvania to see my family. I have my Ethics final on Monday, but my professor is compassionate and understanding. I'm confident she'll understand if I miss the final and make it up when I get back.

After weighing out my options, I decided to make a couple of juices. Then I would drive to Pennsylvania to see my grandfather and support my grandmother and my dad. In good conscience, I don't feel comfortable not saying goodbye to my grandfather while he is still alive. After making the juices and packing vegetables into a small cooler, I began to prepare for the drive. I know Top can tell we're going on a road trip, because he's getting excited. Once he sees me breaking down his crate, he knows we are going somewhere.

We get in the car and begin the eight-hour journey to Lancaster, PA. I say a prayer as we get on the highway. I have peace about my unexpected visit and I know my family will greet me with love. I know they'll appreciate my concern and support. Road trips give us the time to do a lot of thinking and soul searching. One moment I reminisce about has to do with decision-making. Whenever I have a big decision to make, like an unexpected trip, or something for school or work, I think about something my grandfather told me: if I have peace about whatever decision I conclude, then that is the best choice to make. I would often call him for his advice about a big decision and he would say to me, "Do you have peace about it?" More times than not, I would say, "Yes." Then he would say to me,

"Well, then that's the best decision to make." The reason he would ask if I had peace about it, is because that's our way of God letting us know he's involved in our decision-making.

Now, when I have a decision to make, I always remember what my grandfather asked me. I know I'm making the right decision when I have peace. The wisdom and knowledge grandfather shared with me is priceless. He has a way of making the hardest decisions seem simple. On the drive to Pennsylvania, I reminisce a lot about the moments with my grandfather, dad, and all of my family. My grandfather has been dying slowly for a few years and the added stress has taken a toll on my grandmother, dad, and uncle. I might not be able to do too much, but at least I can be there in case they need an extra hand. I can always cook for them; everyone loves my cooking and food has a way of comforting and bringing people together.

Day 36

Juice: green pepper, spinach, avocado, jalapeño, zucchini, green onion

Bible verses: Matt 9-10, Psalm 70-71

I made it to Pennsylvania just in time and was able to talk briefly with my grandfather. He was barely coherent, but I was happy to say thank you and goodbye. My dad and grandmother were really happy I made the trip to help and show my support. I don't know how long I'm going to visit, but I can tell they're both exhausted and stressed out. My grandfather is in a lot of pain and it's terrible to hear him wake up and begin to moan. The hospice staff has arrived and the nurse wants my grandfather to be comfortable and pass away without as much pain as possible. She examines his condition and explains that we have to give him liquid morphine every hour, instead of every two hours. This means someone has to stay up all night to give him his dose. Tonight, my dad and his girlfriend, Barbara, are going to stay up with him and take turns sleeping and staying awake. My grandmother will get a night of rest and some much-needed sleep.

I spoke with my sister, Natalie, who is going to college in Philadelphia. I surprised her by telling her I was in Lancaster and told her to take the train so I could see her today. The trip takes a little more than an hour and I meet her at the train station. I haven't seen my sister since Thanksgiving, so I'm happy to be goofy and laugh with her, even if it's just for a day. Like a college student, she has a big suitcase of laundry with her, so she can do her laundry at Dad's house. I'm also happy to see her, so I can feed her. I brought a baked mac and cheese dish from Charlotte. I was to bring it to my uncle's house, but I forgot it, so I decided to bring it with me and feed my family. We all sit down at the table and everyone enjoys the dinner. I'm sitting there with my green juice and educating my family on juicing, a juice fast, and what I'm trying to accomplish by doing this fast. It has been over thirty days of juicing and I'm happy that not too many people—only a few college mates and my family—know about it. I want to keep it that way, because it's a personal thing I don't really want to talk about, unless I'm in a position where I have to.

My sister's laundry is finished and it's almost time for her to head back to Philly. Before we leave, we visit with our grandmother and she shows my sister a bunch of old pictures of her and my grandfather together. I've seen them before, but the pictures are new to Natalie. She is really impressed with all of the accomplishments and adventures my grandparents have experienced. Remember, my grandfather was on *The 700 Club* and had a fifteen-minute radio show. My grandparents have met with world leaders, politicians, artists in the entertainment industry, and were also invited to the White House by President Ford and President Reagan. They've lived an extraordinary life.

As my grandmother shares these memories, my sister takes pictures and makes a commemorative video on her iPhone. I'm really impressed with how smart Natalie is and the love she has for my grandparents. The video isn't complete, but she tells me she will edit it on the train and finish it.

Throughout the entire time we're with our grandmother, the phone is ringing off the hook. It seems like everyone in the world is calling to check on my grandfather. I'm awed by the impression he and my grandmother have left on so many people.

Natalie and I head to train station and we say goodbye. I'll see her again for Thanksgiving. I'm so happy to see her and that she got to say goodbye to Grandpa. Suffering makes hearts tender and today, I really feel the love of all my family members.

Day 37

Juice: tomato, celery, avocado, jalapeño, spinach, green onion

Bible verses: Matt 11-12, Psalm 72-73

Everyone is exhausted over the new medication regimen, but it's a necessity. My goal today is to help out as much as I can. That means cooking, cleaning, and being present and available. My first order of business is to make myself a juice. I feel emotionally drained and I need to replenish my body with nutrients. My dad mentioned that he wanted me to make spaghetti, so I decided to begin making the sauce from scratch after I make my juice.

One motto I live by is, "Everyone wins." I like to position myself where everyone can benefit from a choice I make. Cooking is a perfect situation, because I like to cook, it's therapeutic and relaxing for me, it's artistic, and I can be creative. At the same time, everyone benefits, because they get to eat the food I make—so "everyone wins."

I let the sauce cook low and slow. I add ground turkey to make it a meaty sauce and cook Italian sweet sausage. It's going to be a thick and hearty meal, and I know my family will enjoy it.

I spend the rest of my day at my grandmother's. My dad and grandmother live in the same neighborhood, so I can walk to her house. The proximity is important and it makes me feel good to know they're close to each other. My grandfather seems to be content he's not having moments of pain and sleeps for most of the day. This evening, my brother, Karl, has a softball game; so, if my grandfather is content and everyone is okay, I'm going to support my brother and attend his softball game.

Everyone is calm and relaxed, so I decide to attend my brother's game. I arrive at the softball field, and the smell of cut grass reminds me of my childhood in Lancaster County. I haven't been to one of my brother's softball games, so I'm excited to watch. He has been playing in this league for four years now and he enjoys it. It gives us time to catch up and to see him play. Between his turn at batting and playing in the field, we talk about a wide array of matters. Even though I don't get to see my siblings that often, we are all close and always have a good time. We can easily pick things back up from where we left off. His team lost the game, but the important thing is, he had a good time and I'm happy we had this chance to hang out.

On my way back to my dad's house, I see two ambulances outside his home. I'm not sure what's going on, but I'm immediately informed by the neighbors that my dad's refusing to go to the hospital. He fell down early today, but I didn't think it was a big deal at the time. Apparently, he hit his head when he tripped and fell over his dog's outdoor leash. A few years ago, my dad had neck surgery and his girlfriend is taking the proper precautions to make sure he didn't reinjure his neck from the fall. My dad is being obnoxious and is refusing treatment. My grandmother and Uncle Lawrence show up to persuade him to go. My grandmother asks me to go up to her house and take care of my grandpa. My uncle finally convinces my dad to go to the hospital and everyone goes with them. I stay back to watch over my grandfather. They all go to the hospital and I lay in my grandfather's king size bed, watching over him. I give him his medication and I have my own system: I give him a shot, set my alarm for an hour, and close my eyes to get some rest. I keep the Christian television station on as added support for me and my grandfather. I'm listening more than watching and try to get rest between the doses of medicine.

My family arrives home from the hospital. The x-ray concluded that my dad did not reinjure his neck—thank God. Everyone is tired and stressed out. I tell my grandmother to go to bed and I'll stay up tonight to give Grandpa his medication. I'm in the zone and I feel like I can handle the responsibility, since I have my own system. Each hour I get up and go through the procedure. It is now 2 a.m. and I feel like zombie. I can't believe my grandmother, Barb, and dad have been doing this for a week now. But, I can handle it. I'm honored to help.

At 5 a.m. on the third of May, I give my grandfather a shot of morphine and, with a damp, warm cloth, I wash his face. He's sleeping and he looks peaceful. Around 5:30 a.m., I notice my grandfather's breathing has changed—the breaths are becoming slower and fewer. I begin to nod off but, at 5:39 a.m., I wake up in a panic and look over at him. He looks peaceful and still. Something seems different, so I check his pulse. I place my hand over his heart, and then I get up and walk to his side of the bed to check the pulse in his neck. I keep my finger by his nose to check his breathing. I turn the light on and I know right then he has passed away. He finally stopped fighting death and now he looks so content. My grandfather has transitioned to heaven and I cross his arms over his chest, pull his blanket up to his neck, and make him looked dignified. I give my grandpa a kiss on his forehead, get on my hands and knees, and begin to pray. I thank the Lord for bringing my grandpa into my life. I thank Him for finally releasing him from his pain and taking him to Heaven.

I get up and knock on my grandma's bedroom door. She comes out and I give her a hug. She asks me, "Did Grandpa move on to heaven?" After answering her, we both go into his bedroom and pray together. My grandma says goodbye and kisses him.

I receive a text from my dad and I walk down to his house to give my grandma a moment alone with her husband. I want to tell my dad in person. We both go back to my grandparents' and call Uncle Lawrence. We then begin the process of informing relatives and the hospice.

My grandfather was able to pass away in his home with the people he loves. It was even more special, because I was with him, taking care of him on his last night on Earth. At 5:39 a.m. on the third of May, my grandpa passed away. I couldn't be more delighted with God and how he planned this entire event. I'm happy I could be here to help my family. Family really is everything.

Day 38

I didn't make juice today. I barely took in any fluids other than coffee. I'm hopped up on coffee from staying up all night and don't feel like making a juice. I've been awake for over twenty-four hours, but I probably won't sleep at all; I'm not tired. Since my grandfather has passed away, I need to stay strong for my family and help wherever I can. I call my sister and brother while my dad calls my other brother, Tim. I finalize my grandfather's obituary, which I collaborated on with Uncle Floyd. My grandfather's obituary reads:

Obituary
Rev. Floyd Baker

Rev. Floyd Merril Baker Sr. of Lititz, Pennsylvania, has transitioned to his final reward on May 3, 2016 after a long battle with congestive heart failure, diabetes, and other debilitating illnesses. He was born on January 10, 1934 in Oneonta, New York. He was eighty-two years old. He has preceded his wife, Leona, and seven children. Kathy Wilson (deceased), Sandy Smice, Karl Baker, Floyd Baker Jr., Lawrence Baker, Mark Baker, and Jonathon Baker.

He also leaves behind numerous adoring grandchildren and great-grandchildren, whom he has counseled, loved, and shared his faith with. Rev. Baker was a highly-decorated 82nd Airborne Paratrooper, who fought and was wounded in action at Pork Chop Hill. He served two tours in the Korean War. Subsequently, he dedicated his life to the ministry of sharing God's word. He was a faithful pastor, a trailblazing evangelist for The 700 Club, and an Apostle to countless congregations *throughout the United States and many nations around the world.*

His last congregation was Antioch Community Ministries in Summerville, South Carolina. In his final years, he attended New Covenant Christian Church in Lititz, Pennsylvania. Rev. Baker has touched the lives of countless people around the world for over sixty years. He will be greatly and deeply missed. He was a loyal warrior to his nation, a steadfast patriot, and a devoted servant to the Kingdom of God. He will now be able to hear the final words his heart has longed to hear.

His Lord said unto him,

"Well done, thou good and faithful servant: thou hast been faithful over a few things, I will make thee ruler over many things: enter thou into the joy of thy Lord." Matthew 25:21

Day 39

Juice: *spinach, avocado, tomato, green onion, jalapeño*
Bible verses: *Matt 15-16 Psalm 76-77*

I'm heading back to Charlotte this morning. I have to take my final for Ethics. I skipped class on Monday and I need to get back now. My grandfather's funeral is Saturday but, because of how everything worked out, I don't feel like I need to be there. My family understands and they've been supportive. They are happy I unexpectedly came to Pennsylvania and understand I have to get back.

I cook breakfast for my family and we share memories of Grandpa and a few laughs. We're all at peace about his passing and are happy he's no longer suffering. After breakfast, I make juice for the road and say goodbye to everyone. We experienced a lot of intense emotions in this short period and I'm worn out. I'm hoping the eight-hour drive goes by fast.

Top and I get into the car and begin our journey. I'm falling asleep at the wheel through most of the trip. I keep the windows rolled down and the music loud. The weather is gloomy and cold; it feels like a fall morning. My juice has extra jalapeño in it for an added kick—which I need. The spices keep me alert, and I drink it fast. The juice tastes even better than usual, but I think it could be because I haven't had any nutrients for a day now.

We finally arrive in Charlotte. I unload my car, take Top for a quick walk before taking a shower, and I'm in bed by 6:30 p.m. I feel drained but can't fall asleep. I rest my eyes and lie in silence until I finally fall asleep by 12:30 a.m. I pray I wake up rested and focused to take my final.

Day 40

Juice: peaches, broccoli, spinach, apple, honey
Bible verses: Matt 17-18, Psalm 78-79
Weight: 243.3 lb, 44.2 lb loss

I'm back home in Charlotte and I slept great last night. I feel rested but I'm still emotionally worn out. I'm also beginning to feel the effects of my grandfather's death: I'm depressed and angry. I'm happy he's not suffering anymore, but witnessing how my grandfather lived his life makes me resentful toward all the terrible people in the world. I've barely rolled out of bed and I'm already annoyed with human beings. I can tell it's going to be a challenging day, so I immediately begin to pray and ask the Lord to equip me with His full armor.

It's day 40 of my fast and I think about Jesus fasting for forty days. Even though I'll be fasting for a hundred days, Jesus fasting for forty days is more incredible. For forty straight days, He went without food and water. That is intense. He also encountered Satan in human form, trying to tempt Jesus to break His fast and follow Satan. The enemy has challenged me throughout this fast, but God has anointed this fast. I don't know why and I don't know what's going to come of this fast, but I'm going to stay strong and complete this task.

Tomorrow, I'm leaving for Hilton Head Island, South Carolina, to visit my mother for Mother's Day. My aunt, Wanda, is coming to visit as well, and I'm going to prepare a nice gourmet meal for them. Since my mother lives on the beach, I'm hoping this will be a relaxing weekend-vacation. I'm going to spend some alone time on the beach, and pray and see if the Lord reveals anything to me. I don't want to be in a state of depression or resentment through this mourning period. I want to be happy for my grandfather and remember the good times. I know my mother and aunt will try to cheer me up. They're fun, loving, and know how much my grandfather meant to me. We had a close relationship and today, I'm going to remember all the wisdom and love he showed me. I'm going to work hard at being happy today and give thanks to the Lord for forty days of successful fasting, enabling me to break away from the world, and the opportunity to honor God.

Day **41**

Juice: broccoli, radish, tomato, green onion, green pepper, jalapeño, avocado

Bible verses: Matt 19-20, Psalm 80-81

Now I'm heading to Hilton Head Island for the weekend. We should all have a fun weekend. I haven't seen my mom for a while now. I actually don't remember the last time I saw her. She was living in Florida earlier, so it was hard to visit because of our schedules. Now, she's a lot closer and I'll be able to visit her more often.

Ever since my grandfather passed away, I've been seeing the value in close proximity to family. It's important to me that I re-establish a connection with my family. That was one of the reasons I left Austin. I only saw my family once or twice a year and I was becoming lonely. This year, I've already seen my sister, brother, Dad, my uncle, and my paternal grandparents. I'm building memories and good times with all of them.

The drive to Hilton Head Island is only four hours. Top is a trooper and never gets car sick. He loves to travel and is a great travel companion. He usually sleeps in the backseat for most of the ride, while I listen to podcasts of preachers, such as Joel Osteen, Pastor Rick Warren, Charles Stanley, Dr. Joyce Myers, Jentezen Franklin, and T.D. Jakes, just to name a few. Self-improvement is a big part of my life and listening to these podcasts has helped me find an alternative perspective and to look at life through my walk with God. I'm learning to take it one day at a time and not to condemn myself for my past. It's important to learn to let go of past hurts and not to be resentful of the people I love just because they have made mistakes or because of my past mistakes.

Day 42

Juice: *celery, carrot, broccoli, radish, tomato, green onion, green pepper, jalapeño, avocado*

Bible verses: *Matt 21-22, Psalm 82-83*

I wake up to a beautiful, sunny morning. I hear Aunt Wanda's voice; she's the loud and fun aunt, so I'm happy to see her. My mother, Rob, Aunt Wanda, and I go sightseeing and shopping for a Mother's Day meal. I plan to cook for them. Mom and Rob eat clean and healthy, which I love. I decide to prepare a nice seafood meal. I buy scallops, mussels, shrimp, and asparagus and prepare a nice gourmet meal for my family. Everyone is impressed with the taste and quality of the food, and especially how I'm able to prepare the dishes with fresh cilantro, basil, and very little fat.

The rest of the day we relax and sit by the pool. The weekend is a success and relaxing for everyone. I'm happy to have visited my mother; it really made her weekend. She tells me several times how much she's proud of me. I've been praying for God's encouragement and, within the past week of visiting my grandparents, Dad, and now Mom, I'm really shocked how many times I've heard my family express to me how proud they are of me. I've noticed between the two trips how much growth my family is showing. They're growing from the hurt a divorce brings and they're learning to move on. I just want both my parents to be happy and to rely on God.

Day 43

Juice: broccoli, radish, tomato, green onion, green pepper, jalapeño, avocado

Bible verses: Matt 23-24, Psalm 84-85

Today is Mother's Day and I enjoy this Sunday morning by going for a walk with her. I bring Top and my mother is beginning to grow accustomed to him. He is a loveable dog and everyone is always impressed with how well behaved he is. We talk about everything from girls, my siblings, my mother's job, and school. I've also been educating her about juicing and fasting.

The weather is beautiful and several families are enjoying this Mother's Day by going on bike rides and walks as well. Hilton Head is beautiful and everyone I've met has been really nice.

I don't feel like leaving, I just want to sit and relax by the poolside all day. I decide I'm going to stay one more night. I spend the rest of the day sitting at the pool and thinking about the events that took place this past week. It's almost overwhelming and I become emotional. I'm also becoming more depressed and coming to the realization that my grandfather is dead. It's so weird to me; I feel like a part of me has died too. My grandfather gave the best advice and it's hard to believe I can't call him anymore. I used to pray that God wouldn't take Grandpa until I was mature enough in my walk with Him. I don't know if that's an answered prayer. This has taken a toll on me and I'm praying for encouragement and love from God.

Sitting by the pool in contemplation of life during this fast has been good for me, but I know I'm in a funk and just want to cry and sleep. I have to go home in the morning, because my next semester begins soon and I have a paper due, which I haven't even begun.

Day 44

Juice: avocado, green pepper, jalapeño, green onion, broccoli
Bible verses: Matt 25-26, Psalm 86-87
Weight: 242 lb, 45.5 lb loss

The only thing I really want to do today is go to the gym and weigh myself. I'm curious to see how much I've lost. I'm also curious, because I've been traveling this week and I want to see if stress and traveling have had any effect on my weight. Other than that, I don't want to do much today. I have class this evening.

I begin a new semester every eight weeks at Montreat College's Adult Graduate Program and the semesters are intense. I have a reflective paper due in a few hours and I don't think I'll have it completed on time. Actually, I know I'm not going to make the deadline. I'm so tired and the after effects of my grandfather's passing don't seem like they'll go away anytime soon. I'm relying on my professor's grace to give me a pass until tomorrow morning. Dr. Nelson is cool and I had her last semester; she knows how important and impactful my grandfather was to me, so I'm sure she will be compassionate toward my situation.

It's dreadful to leave my bed, all I want to do is watch Amazon Prime all day and be left alone. I'm in a really bad mood; and it's causing me even more irritation that I'm accepting and grieving this way. I thought I'd be happy that my grandfather is no longer suffering and is now in heaven. He would always tell me when he was sick to rejoice over his life and be happy he's in heaven. He would tell me, "Uly, I don't want you to be upset; I want you to rejoice!" When he was in his last stages, I would pray for God to take him, so he wouldn't have to suffer anymore. I don't regret it, but I thought I was strong enough in God to not be grieving this way. The grieving process is much more intense than I thought it would be and I just want to get out of this funk. I'm finally beginning to accept that I won't see him again in this lifetime and it's hard to deal with.

Day 45

Juice: *broccoli, avocado, tomato, jalapeño*
Bible verses: *Matt 27-28, Psalm 88-89*

I fully believe decompressing is a must to be at our best. I'm spending my day cleaning, which helps me to decompress; the act of cleaning helps me to clean out negative feelings. On days when I need to fully decompress, I begin my mornings reading my Bible until the word of the Lord jumps out at me and fills me up. Next, I make juice, leave it in the blender, and place it in the refrigerator, so it becomes really cold. Lastly, I start to clean my apartment. I usually begin with the bathroom and move to my living room and kitchen. I add carpet freshener and vacuum the floor when I'm finished cleaning everything. When I'm done, I turn off all electronics, light a sage incense, and take Top for a walk. During the walk, I pray, ask God for forgiveness, and just praise Him in my own way of worship.

When I return to my apartment, the incense is usually finished burning and I can feel the clutter from my mind, body, soul, and home are set back in order. I can now move on to the next task and accomplishments in life. Depending on what Christian you talk to, the next thing I do might seem weird, but I live by it. I go into the shower with a small bottle of anointing oil. I pray over the oil and ask God to use the oil to recharge, renew, and strengthen my anointment. I speak in tongues and pray. When the ritual is over, I feel like a new man—a better man—a humble man who just wants to improve in all areas of life through Jesus Christ.

Day 46

Juice: *tomato, avocado, spinach, jalapeño, green pepper*
Bible verses: *Mark 1-2, Psalm 90-91*

Mark 2:19-22, Jesus is questioned about fasting and he says:

> *Can the friends of the bridegroom fast while the bridegroom is with them? As long as they have the bridegroom with them they cannot fast. But the days will come when the bridegroom will be taken away from them, and then they will fast in those days. No one sews a piece of unshrunk cloth on an old garment; or else the new piece pulls away from the old, and the tear is made worse. And no one puts new wine into old wineskins; or else the new wine bursts the wineskins, the wine is spilled, and the wineskins are ruined. But new wine must be put into new wineskins.*

This speaks to me during this fast, because I believe God is purging me of my past and is transforming my body so that he can "fill me up with new wine." He is going to use me for great things and he wants me to be in my perfect skin. This is both a preparation period and a resting period. The rest part is becoming easy, but the preparation period is challenging. I can endure the suffering of loneliness, shedding of old memories, and moments when I feel the urge to break my fast to eat a cheeseburger. I can endure it. I'm able to face this challenge, because my faith has grown enormously. The clarity I have from not eating solids is revealing God's purpose for my life. I accept that God wants me to be an educator. As a therapist and a professor, He wants me to educate people on faith and God's word. Each of these occupations are becoming easier for me. I comprehend more knowledgeable in my clinical mental health counseling program. I convey what I've witnessed God do in my life though witnessing and cognize becoming a professor. I'm also beginning to distinguish my role in my family.

It's now day 46 and I can feel God working supernaturally. Thank you, Jesus.

Day 47

Juice: *strawberry, banana, coconut water, organic peanut butter*

Bible verses: *Mark 3-4, Psalm 92-93*

Since I began writing this book on fasting, I made up my mind to reveal what's going on in my life and how God is working in me. I wrote I would reveal the Bible verses and the juices I make during this fast. I feel compelled to tell the truth about last week. I didn't give in to eating and I won't, no matter what. But I did backslide when it came to drinking alcohol. On the third of May, when my grandfather died, later that day, I was at my dad's house and I foolishly believed I could bond with him by drinking a beer. I wasn't raised in a normal family and I don't have many ways to bond with my dad other than fishing and hunting. The only other thing I could think of was drinking together. I didn't get falling-down drunk or do anything absurd, but I unwisely thought I could encourage him and help him change the way he communicates with people by drinking with him. Well, of course, it didn't work. The next morning, I didn't feel terrible, but I did feel like he "won" here—I'm claiming Jesus and then I drink. I feel like my dad likes it when I stumble, because he "has no use" for the church or Christians.

During Mother's Day weekend, I repeated this method of bonding with my mom and Aunt Wanda, foolishly thinking I could be an encourager and bond with them—but that backfired as well. I was also mourning at the time and I thought it was easy to just make an excuse and drink my sorrows away. I'm the type of person who is either hot or cold—I don't like lukewarm. My self-treatment used to include alcohol but, through counseling, I found healthy alternatives to deal with my issues. Once I felt I could handle the alcohol responsibly, I would drink only now and then. However, the closer I become to the Lord, the more I don't want to drink. I just don't have the desire anymore. The enemy attacks us when we are weak, tired, and hurt. The enemy only comes to steal, kill, and destroy. He tried to destroy me on two different occasions, but God was with me. Integrity and honesty have a direct correlation to being a man or a woman of God. I feel better sharing this and know I'm growing, because I do not desire to hide my failures.

I hope sharing this helps someone grow just like I am. Thank you, Jesus, for giving me the strength to share my drinking during this fast. Thank you for my growth; thank you for showing me how to take it one day at a time; even though I sometimes feel like a fool for writing during this fast, I thank you, because I know you're going to do something amazing through this book: I thank you for my failures that give hope to someone who's hurting.

Thank you, Jesus, for your encouragement and love. In Jesus's name, Amen.

Day **48**

Juice: peaches, spinach, broccoli, mango, raw honey

Bible verses: Mark 5-6, Psalm 94-95

Blessed is the man whom you discipline, O Lord, and whom you teach out of your law, to give him rest from days of trouble, until a pit is dug for the wicked. For the Lord will forsake his people, he will not abandon his heritage. Psalm 94:13-14

Powerful words in this book.

The days that I'm the most tired, the words of the Bible jump out at me the most. It's easy to become exhausted during a fast, but I've been learning about my body—when to push and when to rest.

Today is a day of rest. This is my first weekend home in two weeks and I want to spend my time wisely—accomplishing schoolwork, resting, and meditating.

I decided to go to the movie theater this early afternoon and watch *The Jungle Book* directed by Jon Favreau. The movie was really awesome. I remember watching the animated version as a child and loving Baloo, the bear. I thought of him as a hip bear that I'd like to hang out with. I had forgotten how Mowgli ended up in the jungle by himself, but this was explained in the new version. After the film, two things occurred to me: Firstly, everyone's interpretation of the Bible is different. Did Jesus really walk on water or is it a metaphor? I believe He really did walk on water, but some disagree. The point I'm trying to make is, we interpret ideas, books, and films differently, but we develop an understanding through communicating different views to one another. We're called to spread the word, not shove our views down people's throats, and then banish them when they don't like those views. I personally believe it's time we get back to the basics and learn how to love one another and communicate to one another in a respectful way. Secondly, is life like a forest or a jungle? We're all in this "jungle" together and we have to survive. During the film, I thought about how the jungle is Earth and all the different animals form our society of different races, genders, religions, and cultures. As the movie shows us, we all need to survive in harmony. We all have a Shere Khan in our life, which is the test, and to defeat the test, we must learn a lot about ourselves, our faith, and become an overcomer—which ultimately builds character.

Day 49

Juice: spinach, peaches, broccoli, mango, honey

Bible verses: Mark 7-8, Psalm 96-97

Workout: squat, bench, triceps, biceps, shoulder press, seated dip, mid row, decline press, pec fly

I wake up feeling energized and wanting to get workout early this morning. I'm going to begin focusing on lifting more than cardio, because I don't want to lose any muscle mass during the rest of this fast. All of my research points to a more sculpted body when we choose to lift instead of focusing solely on cardio. Plus, I don't really like to run unless I'm playing a sport. Running for fun has never really been fun to me, except when I was in the army. I liked running in the morning with my fellow soldiers and hearing the cadence throughout the military base. I sometimes miss the sound of a group united in their steps and in cadence across an entire post. Then again, I'm glad I don't have to do it every single morning.

After my workout, I plan to go to the coffee shop and finish another paper. The new semester has begun and I'm now taking Counseling Skills with Dr. Nelson. She was my professor last semester and I'm glad she's my professor this semester too. I've learned a lot from her and value the knowledge she brings to the class. Her exams are challenging and rigorous, but I know the tough exams will prepare me for when I graduate and have to take the North Carolina State Board exam to become a licensed professional counselor.

I arrive at Amelie's Bakery. I feel upbeat and in the zone to write. I choose to sit at the coffee bar instead of a table. I want to sit up high and people-watch while I write. Sometimes I find inspiration watching a couple or a family. I notice the idiosyncrasies of some of the people and somehow, it helps me find ideas to make my research papers more interesting. An older gentleman sits at the bar, sipping his coffee. We begin to chat and I find out he has arrived from China, where he was a professor for twenty years. He tells me about it and I share with him my aspirations of becoming a professor. We end up talking for about two hours and I learn a lot about becoming an international professor. I think it would be a great adventure and I even express the idea of teaching soldiers who are stationed overseas. I could definitely see myself doing this. It all depends where I am in life when I graduate.

I had a great day and the weather is beautiful. I'm eagerly anticipating day 50 tomorrow and I've purchased a steak and a dozen eggs—not for me but for Top. I'll make him a steak and eggs breakfast, so he can celebrate with me and I can, in some ways, live vicariously through him.

Day 50

Juice: *beets, green onion, jalapeño, spinach, carrot, celery, tomato, avocado*
Bible verses: *Mark 9-10, Psalm 98-99*
Workout: *bench, decline, incline, pec fly, shoulder shrugs, triceps, biceps*
Weight: *238.4 lb, 49.1-lb loss*

The second quarter is over! Praise God, I have now fasted for fifty days! I have surpassed my previous fast of forty-five days and I'm feeling strong.

This morning's service at University City United Methodist Church is special in so many ways. My heart is especially open to receive the message, because today is Pentecost Sunday. Pentecost Sunday is when the Holy Spirit descended upon Jesus's disciples and followers. I'm happy to be in church this Christian holiday morning. For the last two years, I've been learning about the Holy Spirit and how to pray to the Holy Spirit. I'm honored to be fasting on this commemorative day and to have the Holy Spirit in me as I go through the next fifty days.

While at church, Pastor Ron shares who the Holy Spirit is: "Pentecost is the power of the Holy Spirit, which gives us identity, guides us into the fullness of life, cleanses our sins, and sends revival when we are astray." Before the service is over, Pastor Ron makes a compelling statement. "Pentecost power is yours for the asking!" Learning to rely on the Holy Spirit is a process of trust and faith. As I grow in faith, it's becoming easier to call on the Holy Spirit and trust the outcome of what I'm praying for.

After church, I arrive at the gym early this afternoon, ready to hit the gym hard and celebrate this day with an intense workout. Now that I've hit the halfway point, I've decided to incorporate lifting weights for the rest of this fast. Since I've lost a tremendous amount of weight so fast, I don't want to lose any muscle mass. Instead, I want to challenge myself to lift hard and see if I can shed fat but maintain or increase muscle mass. My goal is to become stronger mentally, physically, and spiritually. I believe my spiritual growth has grown enormously during these past fifty days. I've learned to rely on God and praise Him during the good times and the bad.

I've learned that, even though hard times will come, they're all in His glory and they'll bring me closer to Him.

On this day, I imagine how I will feel and look on 4th of July. My glass is half full and I feel like a warrior. I've never felt better in my life. I've decided to rest in solitude as much as possible. Now that my grandfather has passed away, I must learn to speak to God and the Holy Spirit and learn to hear His voice. I anticipate the next fifty days to be challenging, but I will persevere, because I have the Trinity with me and I grow every day in faith.

Day **51**

Juice: watermelon, mango, apple, kiwi, coconut water

Bible verses: Mark 11-12, Psalm 100-101

Workout: cable crossover, low row, lat pulldown, row/rear deltoid, shoulder press

I'm motivated for class tonight. Last week, I wasn't myself and I probably shouldn't have attended class. I was depressed and hurting, but now I feel like I'm getting back to my old self again.

This morning, I arrived at the gym and had a really good workout. I'm pushing my body harder than I have in a long time, but it feels good. However, I can tell I'm not going to be able to push myself all week. After my workout, I feel tired and the shower feels great.

The juice I made today is all fruit. I added coconut water to change it up and get another layer of flavor. Plus, I've mostly been juicing vegetables for a while now and I need a variety when it comes to flavor. I really like the consistency of the mango. It's sweet and creamy, which I think helps fill me up. Whenever I make a juice that is has more of a fruit base, I always drink it a lot faster than a juice made of only vegetables. My body craves sugar and I need the sugar after this workout. I also see a huge change in the way I feel, now that I've lost almost 50 pounds. I'm wearing clothes I haven't worn in a long time and notice how skinny my face and neck look.

Today's workout has put me in a good mood and I carry that over to my evening class. I'm praying that I can stay happy and focus on God's blessings this week.

Day 52

Juice: beets, spinach, apple, watermelon, tomato, jalapeño, green pepper, green onion
Bible verses: Mark 13-14, Psalm 102-103
Workout: Chest press, lat pulldown, shoulder press, triceps press, high row, 20 laps

I now have a workout routine and it feels good. I'm going to the gym daily and either lifting weights or swimming laps, or both.

Today, I swam twenty laps after lifting weights and I had to really push myself to finish the workout. I wanted to quit after ten laps, but I forced myself to be patient and rest for a couple of minutes before pushing myself to complete the last ten laps. I felt even better that I took the time to complete all twenty laps. I enjoy swimming, because water is symbolic of a cleansing agent; swimming works the entire body. Swimming is also a good time for me to be alone, meditate on the day, and pray to the Holy Spirit.

Ever since Pentecost Sunday, I've tried to have a more intimate relationship with the Holy Spirit. At the same time, I believe I'm being attacked by the enemy even more than usual. The enemy is relentless and I've learned that the closer I become with the Lord, the more relentless the enemy is. Sometimes, I believe it's a test to see if I can stay strong in my faith with God and rebuke the enemy out of my life. I'm realizing more and more how much I need this time of rest and solitude. I can feel the breakthrough is right around the corner and I know it has to do with this fast. My physical strength is increasing, but I'm also physically fatigued. I don't think I'll go to the gym for the next two days. I need to know when to rest and when to push myself. Right now, I need to rest.

Day 53

Juice: *tomato, jalapeño, avocado, spinach, celery, carrot, green pepper*

Bible verses: *Mark 15-16, Psalm 104-105*

I plan on resting today and really working on my attitude and mental health. A good way for me to do this is to go back to my art therapy class at the Matthews Art Center. I haven't been to Art Therapy in two weeks now. I'm excited to get back to class and release some emotional baggage through painting.

I arrive at the art center and I'm welcomed by all the veterans with open arms. My art teacher, Eileen, is happy to see me and I'm happy to see her as well. She has been so encouraging to me during this time of loss. She understands I don't really want to paint these days, but encourages me to doodle or sketch just to get used to expressing my feelings in a healthy way.

I sit and talk with my new friend, Tom, who has been in this class for a while, but hasn't really been regular with the classes. We talk and I find out he has been doing missionary work through his church for several years. He shares with me the value of being a missionary and how it has changed his life. He has traveled to Honduras, Africa, and several other countries. He expresses to me the emotional impact it has and how humbling the experience is.

I've become more interested in missionary work as my faith grows. I would like to travel to the Dominican Republic, where my family is from, and help the impoverished children of the country. Today's Bible reading is:

> *Go into all the world and preach the gospel to every creature. He who believes and is baptized will be saved; but he who does not believe will be condemned. And these signs will follow those who believe: In My name they will cast out demons; they will speak with new tongues; they will take up serpents; and if they drink anything deadly, it will by no means hurt them; they will lay hands on the sick, and they will recover. Mark 16:15-18*

Jesus is speaking and, in His own words, explains to His followers that He has given us authority to cast out demons and heal the sick. This Bible passage has never touched me the way it did today. After reading it several times, I actually believe I have the authority to heal the sick in Jesus's name. My power in faith and in Christ becomes stronger each day of this fast. I believe the Lord is speaking through me and even though I'm being attacked immensely, I know God is with me and He will never leave me. He is actually revealing Himself to me during this time and I believe He will continue to reveal himself to me, making my power strong through Him and His name.

Day 54

Juice: avocado, tomato, beets, jalapeño, green pepper

Bible verses: Luke 1-2, Psalm 106-107

I noticed Psalm 106 and 107 both start out with the same passage:

Oh, give thanks to the Lord, for He is good! For His mercy endures forever. Psalm 106:1

Psalm 107 starts with the exact passage. The subtitle for Psalm 106 is Joy in Forgiveness of Israel's Sins and the subtitle for Psalm 107 is Thanksgiving to the Lord for His Great Works in Deliverance. The way I interpret these two passages is, we are to give thanks, because God is good. If nothing else, give thanks for His goodness. His goodness endures forever and whether we are giving thanks for His goodness in deliverance or giving thanks for His goodness in forgiveness, we are to always give thanks.

I sometimes become frustrated, because my timing and God's timing don't always align. I'm learning to give thanks during the waiting period. I'm also learning to give thanks even when I'm upset and hurting. It's not always easy, but I do know I always have something to give thanks for. When I focus on God's goodness and praise Him during the hard times, I've noticed I don't stay upset for too long. God is working in me and He wants me to trust Him when I don't have enough strength, when I'm hurting, and when times are good and I'm happy. I'm to give thanks always, because God is always good. I'm learning to give thanks as soon as my feet hit the floor when I wake up. I am learning to give thanks when I feel defeated. I know God is always with me and I need to put on His full armor daily, because the enemy comes to steal, kill, and destroy. I know this so I must prepare for battle every day. The best way to fight the battle is to give thanks to the Lord during the battle and keep faith for a breakthrough.

Today, I feel strong knowing God's goodness endures forever.

Day 55

Juice: beets, tomato, jalapeño, spinach, celery, carrot, avocado, jalapeño, green pepper, green onion
Bible verses: Luke 3-4, Psalm 108-109
Workout: 20 laps

I'm back to the gym today. I'm still fatigued from the previous workouts of the week. I decide to stay away from the weight room and swim twenty laps in the pool. The cool water feels good against my skin and I meditate while I'm in the water. I think about all the new beginnings in my life. Even though I've lived in Charlotte for a year, it's still brand new to me. I've been enrolled at Montreat College for four semesters, but being back in school is new as well. Not working and living in this season of rest, switching careers is challenging and new as well. The second half of this hundred-day fast is also new. The past five days have been more of a mental challenge than the entire first half of this fast. The enemy has been relentlessly attacking me mentally. Every day has been a battle and I'm becoming a prayer warrior. It also feels like I can no longer feel God's presence. I know He is with me, but it's difficult to hear His voice. However, I will continue to be a prayer warrior.

I call my grandmother for encouragement. She was a pastor along-side my grandfather and she is a valuable resource for God's word and wisdom. We talk for a bit and I share with her my challenges. She gives me great advice on how to pray. She explains to me how in the book of John, chapter 1, explains we are to be a witness of the Light, which is Jesus Christ. I'm trying to be steadfast. I will be steadfast.

I don't believe in coincidences, but I find it funny that today's Bible reading of Luke, chapter 4, is when Satan tempts Jesus. Satan says to Jesus, "If you are the Son of God, command this stone to become bread." But Jesus answers, "It is written, Man shall not live on bread alone, but by every word of God." I'm feeling tempted by Satan. He tempts my flesh to give into lust, alcohol, and pornography, but I'm fighting it by praying and rebuking him. I've been praying so hard that I feel crazy reciting some of these prayers aloud repeatedly. I know God is with me and this is part of the fasting process.

Satan is a faithful enemy, who will relentlessly attack when we are weak, tired, and wounded. Today, I feel like I'm all of the three, but God is with me and I will prevail in my battle against Satan. God has given me authority to fight off Satan in His name. I will remain steadfast and victorious, because God is with me. I will praise God's name while I am attacked and I will praise His name when He lifts my name and blesses me.

Day 56

Juice: beets, green onion, green pepper, jalapeño, avocado

Bible verses: Luke 5-6, Psalm 110-111

Workout: adjustable pulley, squat, low row, lat pulldown, mid row, pec fly, seated dip, leg extension, leg curl

I wake up this morning feeling better than yesterday. I immediately pray and put on the full armor of God. I'm ready for battle today and no longer feel weary from the devil's schemes. I'm up for the challenge and ready to fight.

I arrive at the gym and begin my workout. Instead of listening to music, I listen to Christian podcasts. I'm strengthening and feeding my spirit by listening to these Christian podcasts. I'm also becoming physically and mentally stronger at the same time.

I complete a full-body workout. I like doing full-body during workouts, because they never bore me. A lot of trainers and experts recommend training only one body part during a workout, but I prefer my way better. I believe, with this fast, working out, and reading the Bible verses, it all comes down to what's best for me. With all three, you can tweak it to your own as long as you're getting something out of it daily—that's all that matters. I don't explain how many cups of each ingredient I use or go into extensive detail about my workouts all the time, because I want the reader to use this as no more than a guide. Ultimately, we have to do what's best for us.

I focus today on being a prayer warrior, not letting Satan into my mind, and diligently finish a project for my Counseling Skills class. I have an extensive project—a chart of the twelve major theories we're learning—I have to complete by Monday. I end up uptown at Amelie's Bakery after my workout. The coffee shop is busy and I find a place at the coffee bar to sit before beginning my assignment. The project is making me tired before I even begin. I buckle down and order the strongest coffee they have and force myself to work through the stress and the mental fatigue. Lately, I've been feeling more weary than usual. It's a combination of a spiritual battle as well as an emotional and physical battle. After three cups of Café Allongé, I complete my theories chart and bask in the glory that I've finished the project. All of my homework is complete for this week and it feels good to have killed procrastination once again. Procrastination hasn't lurked around the corner either. Instead, I'm more energetic about completing my weekly tasks.

I spend the rest of the day resting. Even though I had three cups of coffee, I'm tired. I feed my spirit by watching several Christian programs on the TBN. It seems like every preacher is talking to me and me alone. The sermons really helped to relax me and settle my spirit in God's love and favor.

Day 57

Juice: beets, carrots, celery, avocado, green pepper, jalapeño
Bible verses: Luke 7-8, Psalm 112-113

In Luke, chapter 6, Jesus speaks about loving our enemies. This has always been a challenge for me. Instead of loving my enemies, I have hated and resented them. Now, more than ever, I'm accepting that some people in my life and those who have exited will be my enemy. If I can't win them over, I can pray for them. It's challenging to pray for people who have hurt me, shed light only on the embarrassing or bad things I've done, or wished me evil.

I read Luke, chapter 6, a couple of times and began to pray for the people who are no longer a part of my life—old high school friends who I grew apart from, family members who I don't speak to, drinking buddies, and ex-girlfriends. It's hard to pray for my "enemies," because I'll never know if my prayers did anything for them. I guess that's why it's called a selfless act.

> But I say to you who hear: Love your enemies, do good to those who hate you, bless those who curse you, and pray for those who spitefully use you. To him who strikes you on the one cheek, offer the other also. And from him who takes away your cloak, do not withhold your tunic either." Luke 6:27-29

When I read this passage, it shows how humble Jesus is. The pride, anger, and resentment are what stop us from loving our enemies. I want to be at peace so I can love and pray for my enemies. I'm going to carefully meditate on this passage and see what God reveals to me. I know I need to humble myself more, not react to hurtful words of others and, instead of lashing out, be quiet, be still, and know God is with me.

Day 58

Juice: avocado, beets, jalapeño, celery, carrot, spinach, green pepper, green onion
Bible verses: Luke 9-10, Psalm 114-115
Workout: bench press, lat pulldown, chest press, mid row, pec fly, shoulder press, biceps, seated dip, low back, triceps
Weight: 235.8 lb, 51.7 lb loss

I'm extremely happy with my results. I can't believe I've lost over fifty pounds. That's an awful lot of weight and I feel so much better.

Today, I had a good workout, but I still feel anxious about the rest of this fast. I'm ready for it to be over. I feel like I have the weight of the world on my shoulders. I want to make God proud by sticking it out and completing His task.

I'm trying to learn to stop being so hard on myself. Even though I've fasted for almost sixty days, I feel like I'm not doing enough to change my surroundings and experience a breakthrough. Maybe that's what God is trying to teach me. I can't do anything but trust in God and have faith. I'm trying too hard to make Him happy and I need to remember He is already happy with me. Whether I'm at my best or my worst, God still loves me. We fall into guilt and condemnation when we sin and make mistakes. I'm learning through this fast that God is pleased with me and He couldn't love me more, no matter how many days I fast. I plan to spend the day reflecting on all the blessings God has given me and stop worrying about whether I'm pleasing Him or not. God is stretching me to have faith in His grace and stop worrying about making mistakes.

Day 59

Juice: mango, kiwi, apple, watermelon
Bible verses: Luke 11-12, Psalm 116-117

My energy is low today and I plan on taking an off from the gym. Rest is just as important as working out and in some ways, it's more important while I fast.

I've been feeling restless for some time and I don't know why. It seems like all the newness in my life has become overwhelming and I need a release. I want to take a vacation but, since I can't enjoy eating, what's the point? Today is one of those days where I wish I could just run away to a place where I don't have to worry about school, looking for a job, or learning to adapt to my environment. I also feel like a worrier. I'm worrying about all of these things too much and I need to give them over to God today. God doesn't ask us to simply withdraw; fear goes away when we face it head on.

Embracing the newness of life and facing my fears are hard when I try to do them my own. I'm learning to give my fears and worries over to God. Conquering life is the ultimate goal for all of and conquering our fears helps us to embrace life. I also know that the enemy attacks us the hardest when we're tired, hurt, or doubting God. It might not seem like I'm doubting God, but when I look at the big picture, that's exactly what I'm doing. I don't doubt God's power, but I'm doubting if and when I'll experience the breakthrough I need. I know God is with me and I know He's using all of this for the greater good. Sometimes, being positive is hard and being negative is easy. Right now, I need to fight through the pressure and become a prayer warrior.

Day 60

Juice: beets, green onion, tomato, jalapeño, celery, carrots, avocado

Bible verses: Luke 13-14, Psalm 118-119

Today is another day of rest and learning to relax. I don't plan on going to the gym for the rest of the week. I probably won't go back until the Tuesday after Memorial Day. I want to rest my body, mind, and soul.

I'm feeling the attacks of the enemy. The enemy will attack suddenly or subtly, and lately, it has been a little bit of both. I'm at my wit's end with God and finding myself. I'm even doubting whether I should still be on this fast. One day, it seems like God is with me and the next, it doesn't. I feel the enemy a lot clearer than I feel God.

I'm also beginning to doubt whether or not I should continue writing my feelings and emotions down. I don't know why I'm still writing; maybe God's hand is on me and I just don't realize it today. I've grown tired and weary, and the only thing that's keeping me going is, I'm on a mission and I can't quit my mission.

Day **61**

Juice: green pepper, avocado, jalapeño, tomato

Bible verses: Luke 15-16, Psalm 120-121

Yesterday, I spent most of the day in misery and today doesn't seem to be much better. Temptation is clawing at my back and neck and seeping into my mind. My flesh feels raw in spirit and it feels like a dozen demonic creatures are attacking me. I'm thinking about all the sin I've committed and trying to rationalize if that's why I'm miserable. I thought the days were going to get better, but they aren't. For some reason, the days are getting worse.

I feel like the attacks have been daunting since my grandfather passed away. He is the glue to our family's spiritual growth and now that he's not here, the attacks have been getting stronger and stronger. I believe God is testing me once again. Can I stay faithful in the times of these severe attacks? I'm becoming maddened with frustration and wondering where God is. The thought of giving up is at the front of my mind, but I still can't give up. I'm going to rest all day and see if something changes.

Day  62   *Bible verses:* Luke 17-18, Psalm 122-123

I feel like I'm going to faint. My emotions are high and erratic and I have no sense of time; I don't know what day it is. I have a lot of schoolwork and projects to complete and I've only completed one of them. I don't know how I'm going to accomplish another paper or project when I'm feeling like this. Temptation isn't gnawing at my neck anymore; instead, it has fully seeped into my mind and raised my anger to another level. I don't feel like myself. It feels like I'm possessed and God is far away from me. I hope these attacks will soon come to an end. I can only imagine what Jesus went through on his forty-day fast. The enemy had been attacking him since the beginning of his fast. He even tempted Jesus by taking him to the top of the world and claiming that he would give him the kingdom of the world. Jesus wasn't juicing and he didn't have food or water, either. Jesus felt emotions just like we do. He was God in the form of a man, but he still had a man's emotions, which He had to fight to not sin. The thought of this humbles me, but now I'm doubting school. I've become completely overwhelmed with stress and negative emotions, and I keep praying Jesus will help me through the rest of my fast. I'm praying for a breakthrough and that this fast releases supernatural power with God.

I was so weak today that I couldn't make any juice. I barely consumed any liquids. I'm praying God's power once again takes over.

Day 63

Juice: spinach, radish, green, red, yellow, and orange peppers, avocado
Bible verses: Luke 19–20, Psalm 124–125

It's Saturday morning and I can't take one more day of this torture. I start my day differently by putting on the full armor of God and reciting Bible verses, which are usually a part of my daily rituals. I haven't read them the past couple of days, because the demonic attacks have been so strong that I almost gave up.

I decide to not let Satan's attacks get through God's armor. God's mercy is new every morning and I'm fighting the enemy before he starts attacking me. I begin on the offense to put Satan on the defense. I also renew my mind and recharge my anointing. I repent for my sins and begin to praise God for His blessings. I praise Him for my family, my school, my home, my dog, the roof over my head, and my health. I begin to praise Him for everything.

I spend the rest of the day resting in God's word and watching Christian pastors on TBN. I'm not going to condemn myself, because Jesus forgives me when I repent. I forgive myself for doubting God these past few days, and I renew my vows to God, as well as the reasons I'm fasting. I'm proud of myself for not giving in to temptation to eat food and not believing it would be fine to simply begin a new fast. Instead, I remain steadfast and continue to fight off the devil.

I'm more powerful than Satan, because of the blood of Jesus Christ. I keep praying, reading my Bible, and listening to what the pastors are preaching. I begin to feel Satan's grip loosen and feel the love of Jesus. Jesus has overcome the world. He hasn't promised us an easy journey, but he overcame the world and shed his blood was shed for us.

Day 64

Juice: *red, green, yellow, and orange peppers, avocado, radish, spinach*
Bible verses: *Luke 21-22, Psalm 126-127*

I lay on my couch most of yesterday, listening to pastors on television preach while I prayed. But today, I'm going to my local church to receive the word of God. I'm regaining my strength, but I can feel I'm not fully back to myself yet. I decide to take part in communion. I don't feel anything right away and that's normal, but I know when taking part in communion, you reaffirm your relationship with God. I said at the beginning of the fast that I would partake in communion only because it will strengthen me for the journey of the fast through faith in Jesus Christ.

It's Memorial Day weekend and I see my neighbor's barbecuing. I can smell the meats cooking on the grill, but I stay strong. It doesn't bother me at all and that's how I know my strength has come back. My strength is back because of the power of prayer, my faith in Jesus Christ, communion, and searching for God wholeheartedly. My strength in Jesus Christ will get me through this fast and I'm happy that I'm diligent in seeking God. I've received His strength.

Most people are barbecuing today and hanging out with family. I spend the majority of the day the same way I spent my Saturday. I continue to listen to the pastor's messages on television, pray, and read my Bible. I know my strength is back, but I want my armor of God to be stronger than ever. I'm breaking generational curses, which isn't easy. I'm changing the spiritual makeup of my future children through this fast. I'm confident in the rest of this fast; staying diligent in God's word, praying, and listening to God's messages will get me through the rest of the days. I'm thankful for God's grace, love, peace, and protection. God is with me.

Day 65

Juice: *green, red, yellow, and orange peppers, radish, avocado, spinach*

Bible verses: *Luke 23-24, Psalm 128-129*

THIS IS THE KING OF THE JEWS.

Those words were written on the cross Jesus was crucified on. While He was hanging there with two criminals, He was blasphemed again. One of the criminals said to Him, "If You are the Christ, save Yourself and us." It's not enough that He was beaten, tortured, mocked, spit on, and ripped apart. But, in His last dying moments, a criminal who hung crucified next to Jesus, blasphemed Him. The crucifixes and pictures we see of Jesus show Him in a way that is completely different from what is factually presented in the Bible. They have Him looking sober in a small loincloth, when in actuality, his body was ripped open and hung naked. The actual event compared to the pictures we often see is contradictory and does not represent the unbearable punishment Jesus faced.

When I read this, it reminds me of kicking a man while he's down. Even after all those beatings, he was still mocked by a criminal. Jesus, God in a man's body, did all this and has given us the authority, through the blood He shed, to have power over evil forces. The temptation I've felt the last few days is nothing in the big scheme of things. I need to remember that Satan is a loyal advisory, who will stop at nothing to destroy our mind, body, soul, and spirit. I must fight even harder for the rest of this fast.

I feel strong and confident after a few days of a tempted spirit. I'm relentlessly confident. I'm strong and positive. I owe all of these positive emotions to becoming a prayer warrior and for diligently reading my Bible. The full armor of God is on and God is with me. I will be courageous. I will be rich in the Holy Spirit and I will be rich in faith. Thank you, Jesus, for making me battle tested.

Day 66

Juice: spinach, radish, avocado, green, red, yellow, and orange peppers
Bible verses: John 1-2, Psalm 130-131
Workout: lat pulldown, decline press, seated dip, pec fly, lower back, triceps, row, upper and lower cable crossover

I'm finally back to full strength and this experience has brought me closer to the Holy Spirit than I ever expected. I've been praying to the Holy Spirit more than ever and I believe I've surpassed several spiritual levels. I've built and established a relationship with the Holy Spirit that I can't put into words. I'm reflecting on this fast and thus far, I can imagine what the rewards will be. God always blesses us more than we imagine and I'm most proud of the generational curses and relationships that are building with my future children. Knowing that I'm establishing Christ in them is powerful and groundbreaking.

This evening, I was watching Pastor Guillermo Maldonado on TBN. He was preaching a powerful message and I began to take notes. His message was on "How to Fight the Enemy." It was powerful and exactly what I needed to hear to recharge my strength. These are the points he made:

> "We need to take authority in the name of Jesus. We need to crucify our flesh. We need to restrain our flesh. After that, we need to exercise self-control. We must be continually filled with the Holy Spirit."

This is how you fight off the enemy. It was a powerful message. I'm going to fight off the enemy through these notes and see what type of peace I begin to have in my life. I feel great and I'm stronger than ever. Just now, I've realized the power of what we let into our mind through television and music. If I were watching something other than TBN tonight, I would have missed this powerful message. It takes discipline to not give in to the desires of the flesh—to not watch what we know is not healthy for us or does not feed us emotionally and spiritually.

Day 67

Juice: *green peas, corn, Brussels sprouts, broccoli, jalapeño, red, yellow, and orange peppers, avocado, tomato, basil*
Bible verses: *John 3-4, Psalm 132-133*
Workout: *10 laps*

I wake up feeling excited, because I have my art therapy class this afternoon. I haven't been to class in two weeks and I'm excited to see everyone. I wake up early and head to the gym. My muscles are tired, so I'm only going to swim ten laps. I just want to be in the pool, swim ten intense laps, and leave. I've learned to listen to my body and I believe that is all I need as exercise for the day.

The class is having a potluck, since we're having our art exhibition this Sunday. It's called "Art by Vets." Eileen has put this together. The art program is supported by the Town of Matthews and the organization, Flags Across the Nation. I'm really excited for the art exhibit; it's my first time showcasing my art. Even though I'm novice painter, I'm proud of the four paintings that will be displayed.

Since we're having a potluck, I've decided to make a homemade gourmet pizza for the class. I've mastered the art of making dishes without being tempted to try it or taste it for flavoring. Cooking is another form of art for me and plating dishes is rewarding. I made a gluten-free pizza with roasted tomatoes, pepperoni, and spinach.

I show up at the Matthews Art Center and I'm greeted by smiling faces when I surprise the class with the pizza. The pizza was a big hit. Sharing with the class how I made it and how I can transform it into a healthy dish feels great.

Eileen has been an amazing encourager during my mourning process. Her mother is sick and is being cared for, so we have a mutual connection. Today, I prayed for peace for Eileen and her mother, and that the Lord removes the hurt and ailments her mother is suffering from.

Everyone in the class has been encouraging to me and I've learned something from each person. Curt is a photographer and he shared with me some cool places to go camping on the beach. Imogene is a hunter, so we talked about where to hunt in North Carolina. She told me how they have turkey shoots, which is when you shoot for prizes. Kimberly has taken up dog sitting and said she would watch Top for me if I ever wanted to take a weekend trip. Felecia and I talk about her son, who is in the film industry. Don is just a really nice guy. He shares with me techniques and pricing for my art. As I write this, I see how many encouragers I have in my life. We might only meet once a week, but the rewards are monumental. I pray for the entire class that they all have peace in their lives.

I get home and decide to look up the beaches Curt told me about. I decide to book a tent space for July 4th through July 6th. I'm going to spend my hundredth day of fasting at the Myrtle Beach campground at Myrtle Beach State Park. It's going to be Top and me on the beach. Top likes the beach. I took him when my mom lived in Florida and he was six months old. I immediately purchase a tent on amazon and begin to research the Myrtle Beach State Park area.

I've been imagining my first meal. I know what I'm going to make. I imagine some of the vegetables I've been juicing, accompanied by brown rice and a whole fish. I believe that's the kind of meal Jesus would eat. I plan to get up at sunrise to begin cooking. While the fish is grilling, I'll partake in communion. Afterward, I'll take the dish I made, walk to the beach, and enjoy the meal while watching and meditating by the ocean. That sounds amazing to me for my first meal as a new and improved man of God.

Day 68

Juice: green peas, corn, Brussels sprouts, broccoli, jalapeño, red, yellow, and orange peppers, avocado, tomato, basil

Bible verses: John 5-6, Psalm 134-135

I've decided to take a day trip to Montreat College in Montreat, North Carolina. I have a paper I have to complete and I thought it would be nice to write in the mountains today.

During the drive, I'm consumed with negative emotions. I'm feeling overwhelmed with school, looking for a job, and maintaining this fast. Now that it's summer, I want to barbecue and enjoy the summer just like everyone else. Unfortunately, I don't have the luxury of quitting this fast. I'm on a mission and my faith is the most important aspect of my life. I quickly crucify my flesh and keep doing it over and over until I feel the Holy Spirit fill me up with his love and peace.

Sometimes, God will ask us to do something that sounds absurd and impossible. I believe he does it so we can grow. More times than not, he asks us the impossible, so we can be a witness to someone else. I believe this fast is just that. I'm sharing my testimony with the world about a fast—the ups and downs and the emotional rollercoaster a person goes through during a fast. I'm sharing my spiritual walk and how the Holy Spirit is leading me. Every day is a challenge but every day, God gives us the strength to conquer the day. I need to stay focused on God's promise and not my problem. I need to know that His mercy is renewed every morning.

I arrive at Montreat and the mountains are beautiful. I stop by the library and check out the campus before heading to a coffee shop in Black Mountain. The Dripolater Coffeehouse is a cool little coffee shop with the perfect backdrop for writing. I begin to write and the words are flowing. I complete my assignment quickly and I spend the rest of the day walking around Black Mountain.

On the drive back, I feel peace and harmony.

Day 69

Juice: green peas, corn, Brussels sprouts, broccoli, spinach, jalapeño, red, yellow, and orange peppers, avocado, basil

Bible verses: John 7-8, Psalm 136-137

The Promise of the Holy Spirit:

> *If anyone thirsts, let him come to Me and drink. Whoever believes in Me, as the Scripture has said, 'Out of his heart will flow rivers of living water.' John 7:38*

My relationship with the Holy Spirit is growing daily. I'm conscience of the Holy Spirit's presence in my life and I'm trying not to grieve the Holy Spirit through sinning. I'm human, so I won't always get it right, but realizing I'm trying to live righteously is growth in itself. God's mercy is new every morning and through this fast, I've learned not to condemn myself if I make mistakes. Keeping the Lord's name in worship throughout the day has been a huge asset to my mental focus. Instead of rebuking the enemy, I'm learning to keep praising the Lord and the Holy Spirit.

Today is a relaxing day. I take Top to the dog park and hang out with some people there. Top and I stayed at the park longer than usual, because I was having a really good conversation with one of my friends. The park was packed and Top got to run around and play with other dogs. Everyone loves Top; he has a great personality and I've raised him to be social with people and other animals. When I take him out in the mornings, we go on a walk. This time is spent praying, worshiping, and thanking the Holy Spirit for being a part of me. This has become a daily ritual for several weeks and I look forward to the morning worship.

Looking back on the past sixty-eight days, I can see now why God has given me this time of rest. It's so I can learn how to put Him first and learn how to worship, in the good times and the bad times.

Day 70

Juice: green peas, corn, Brussels sprouts, broccoli, spinach, jalapeño, red, yellow, and orange peppers, avocado, basil
Bible verses: John 9-10, Psalm 138-139

Though I walk in the midst of trouble, You will revive me; You will stretch out Your hand against the wrath of my enemies, And Your right hand will save me. Psalm 138:7-8

Every morning, I recite the Jabez prayer for all of the people in my life. I'm trying to pray for more and more people who I can think of and believe that the power of prayer works. Some of us don't always have someone to pray for us. I'm aware of this, so I try to get to know the people in my life; that way, I'll know how to pray for them. I don't let them know I'm praying for them, but God knows and that's what matters. I don't share it with them, because I don't want to be egotistical and make it about me. It's for them.

It's Saturday and I'm driving to McDowell Arts Center in Matthews, NC to help my art therapy class set up for our exhibit. I'm excited to be involved in an art exhibit for veterans. I arrive and help hang paintings and make labels for price tagging the art. The energy of our class is amazing.

Eileen is a great person. She has been an art therapy instructor for veterans for several years now. She has a huge heart and calm spirit. She's going through a lot with her mother's illness and I continually keep her in my prayers.

I've been praying for everyone in the class. As a veteran myself, it's hard to find like-minded people to talk with. I consider myself a strong person, but I'm human and have moments when I break down or just feel emotional. I keep that in mind because, if I'm going through something, there's probably another veteran going through a difficult moment as well.

I've learned a lot from the people in this class. Mainly, I've learned how to be at peace through these great people. Thank You, Father, for bringing these amazing people into my life. I've been praying the Lord brings me good people and now my art is in an exhibit with an entire class of veterans. God is amazing and will always bless us beyond our expectations.

Day 71

Juice: green peas, corn, Brussels sprouts, broccoli, spinach, jalapeño, red, yellow, and orange peppers, avocado, basil
Bible verses: John 11-12, Psalm 140-141

I've been making the same juice for some time now and I love it. There's something about this mixture of vegetables that I really enjoy. The peas mixed with jalapeño, avocado, and basil is a great taste. I added the basil randomly when I cooked a pizza for my art therapy class. I had basil left over, so I thought to put it in one of my juices and see how it tastes. The result was amazing and I'll continue to add basil until I run out. I might buy more and keep it as part of this juice mixture since it's so good.

I decide to skip the traditional service and attend the contemporary church service instead. The service was much different, but I felt the Lord led me to the later service. I really enjoyed the worship and service, and Pastor Chad's message was exactly what I needed to hear. I had an awesome time, the music was great, and I think I'm going to start attending the contemporary service more often. I saw how I worshiped and want to continue that experience.

After the service, I go home and relax until the "Art by Vets" exhibit begins. I can't wait to see what type of turnout we have. I arrive at the Art Center and there are a lot of people admiring our art. The mayor of Matthews arrives and picks his favorite and the Community Center picks its favorite as well. None of my paintings were picked, but I'm happy my work was a part of the exhibit. The paintings they picked were fantastic and well deserving of recognition. I had a great time with my new friends and I'm happy to be a part of healthy relationships and healthy ways to express my emotions. God is awesome. God is with me.

Day 72

Juice: *green peas, corn, Brussels sprouts, broccoli, spinach, jalapeño, red, yellow, and orange peppers, avocado, basil*
Bible verses: *John 13-14, Psalm 142-143*
Workout: *lat pulldown, decline press, seated dip, pec fly, lower back, triceps, row, upper and lower cable crossover, 20 laps*
Weigh in: *227.2 lb, 60.3 lb loss*

I woke up early, went to the gym, and had a great work out. I also swam 20 laps in the pool. After working out, I weighed myself and my weight was 227.2 pounds. I was right: last week, the scale was wrong at the Dowd YMCA. Now, I know to weigh myself at the University City YMCA from now on. I know they calibrated the scale at Dowd, but members of the gym have been complaining that it's still incorrect. At least I know the correct weight now and I'm still happy that I've lost 60.3 pounds in seventy-two days. My neighbors have made positive comments about me and I've been able to share with them my fasting experience and how God is working in my life.

Many people have commented that I have a genuine ability to witness God without sounding like a religious freak. That is probably the best compliment I can receive. All I do is share how God has worked in my life. I share who I was in the past, the events that led to my encounter with Jesus, and what he has done to transform me into the man I am today. My reputation as an open book is important for people to see that God can use anyone. Like I mentioned earlier, He usually uses the person you least expect. I believe that is how he is using me.

I'm back in class this week and I'm so ready for this semester to be over. May was the roughest month I've had since living in Charlotte and this semester, there is a lot of course work. I can't wait to move on to a new course, a new professor, and learn a new topic. God is with me and He will anoint me each day for the task at hand. I feel the Holy Spirit's presence and I've been feeling content and at peace. Thank you, Jesus.

Day **73**

Juice: *green peas, corn, Brussels sprouts, broccoli, spinach, jalapeño, red, yellow, orange peppers, avocado, basil*
Bible verses: *John 15-16, Psalm 144-145*
Workout: *20 laps*

I'm only forty-eight hours away before third quarter is complete! I am happy about hitting another milestone and close to end of this mission God has me on. I begin researching and working on my last presentation for this course. I usually take Tuesday as a personal day to decompress from a four hour Monday night class but today I am diligent and wanting to finish this project early so I can relax the rest of the week. I'm working on the project with my friend Tia. She and I are like-minded people in this cohort and I have turned to her for advice and for venting throughout this semester. She has been a huge help to my mental focus and finding clarity throughout this semester. I am thankful the Lord is using her to help me and has brought an encourager in this cohort.

After a couple of hours of working on the project I take a break and my mom and I speak on the phone for several hours. We haven't talked like that in a long time and it was good to hear her voice and talk about a wide range of topics. I am happy God has answered the prayer of repositioning her closer to me. I share with her that I plan to visit the weekend after 4th of July. I can't wait to visit Hilton head and go to dinner for the first time in over 100 days to one of my favorite restaurants, Hudson's Seafood House on the Docks. I love that place. It's right on the water and the last time I was there I was with my mom and sister and Rob. We had an awesome time and the food is excellent. I was going to wait until my birthday but I don't want to wait that long to eat their amazing food. There is light at the end of the tunnel. Growing in the Holy Spirit has been amazing and I hope to be the catalyst to the rest of my family and help them on their spiritual walk with Christ. Thank you, Jesus.

Day 74

Juice: green peas, corn, Brussels sprouts, broccoli, spinach, jalapeño, red, yellow, and orange peppers, avocado

Bible verses: John 17-18, Psalm 146-147

I woke up early this morning, so I could barbecue chicken for my art therapy class. We're meeting at Eileen's house and I informed the class I would smoke some chicken for everyone. Even though I'm not eating, barbecuing is one of my favorite pastimes. Cooking for them is an excuse for me to relax and barbecue. I even purchase pecan wood chips so I can captivate the wood flavor. The chicken has been marinating in a liquid brine for three days and then in a dry rub for twenty-four hours. I'm hardcore when it comes to barbecuing, so I'm trying to captivate as much flavor as possible. I hope the pecan wood smoke comes through in the chicken and that everyone likes the taste.

I arrive at Eileen's home and she has a beautiful house, decorated with the art pieces of so many of her students. She has pieces by her father and mother as well. It's a warm home and I really needed to feel this positive energy.

I'm working on a project for my class and it has been frustrating. So, taking a break from researching and writing feels great. One of the artists, Paul Gianni, is giving a demo on painting portraits. He uses Curt in his demo, because he wants to paint someone with a beard. It's fascinating to watch him paint; he makes it look so easy. We are all mesmerized with his ability to paint and his techniques.

The afternoon was great and the art therapy session is over. While I head back home, I begin to feel the attacks of the enemy. I begin to feel temptation creeping back into my life the way I felt it a couple of weeks ago. I stay strong and go into prayer mode, fighting off the enemy. Now that I'm getting close to the finish line, the attacks aren't as subtle. Instead, they hit like a sledgehammer and the attacks are fierce. I'm fighting off the temptation to give in to eating and drinking. I'm going to be courageous and keep on the good fight. God is with me and I won't let Him down.

Day 75

Juice: green peas, corn, Brussels sprouts, broccoli, spinach, jalapeño, red, yellow, and orange peppers, avocado
Bible verses: John 19-21, Psalm 148-150
Weigh in: 227.2 lb, 60.3 lb loss

The third quarter is over! I have now fasted for seventy-five days and I look and feel great. The last book of Psalms has the subtitle, Let All Things Praise the Lord.

> *Praise God in His sanctuary; Praise Him in His mighty firmament! Praise Him for His mighty acts; Praise Him according to His excellent greatness! Praise Him with the sound of the trumpet; Praise Him with the lute and harp! Praise Him with the timbrel and dance; Praise Him with stringed instruments and flutes! Praise Him with loud cymbals; Praise Him with clashing cymbals! Let everything that has breath praise the Lord. Praise the Lord! Psalm 150:1-6*

The book of Psalms is known as the book of praise, because just about every chapter has a reference to praising God during the good, the bad, and the ugly times of our life. Through this fast, I'm learning to praise God no matter what the circumstance are in my life; no matter the thoughts going on in my head; and no matter if I'm having a good day or bad day.

It's crazy to think I've been fasting for seventy-five days. It's even crazier to realize I'm finally on the last quarter. God is with me and I feel His presence. I have cried out to Him during these seventy-five days. I have doubted His presence at times, but I have worshiped Him throughout. My faith has grown. I have a stronger relationship with the Holy Spirit and I've lost 60 pounds. Praise God! God is with me!

Day 76

Juice: *green peas, corn, Brussels sprouts, broccoli, spinach, jalapeño, red, yellow, and orange peppers, avocado*
Bible verses: *Job 1-2, Acts 1-2*

The book of Job is a book about a man named Job, who had it all and then lost it all. He loses his family, wealth, health, and family. He doesn't understand why he lost everything and asks why. The crazy part about this book is God and Satan discuss testing Job by taking everything from him. God debates with Satan that Job will stay loyal, while Satan believes Job will turn on God. In the end, of course, God is right. Job goes on a traumatic journey but, in the end, he realizes that God is sovereign.

I've had moments where I don't realize God is sovereign and I think he's picking on me or hazing me. At times, life is difficult for all of us, but those tough times actually strengthen our faith; they make us realize that God is sovereign. The book of Acts is written by Luke and records Jesus's last words, known as the Great Commission. Acts is about Jesus's followers and how they took the Great Commission seriously during their journey.

> *But you shall receive power when the Holy Spirit has come upon you; and you shall be witnesses to Me in Jerusalem, and in all Judea and Samaria, and to the end of earth. Acts 1:8*

It calls for his followers to be witnesses and to share the Gospel. They are to go to the remote places on earth and witness what Jesus Christ has done. It isn't always easy to share the Gospel, especially in present society. We have suffered so many traumatic events, terrorist acts, and wars. I'm learning to be a witness and it's becoming easier. But, at times, it's still challenging when you're among those who have not seen the light.

Day 77

Juice: *green peas, broccoli, spinach, jalapeño, green peppers, avocado*

Bible verses: *Job 3-4, Acts 3-4*

Now that I have a stronger relationship with the Holy Spirit, I enjoy reading about Him in the beginning of Acts. I'm trying to take my relationship with the Holy Spirit seriously and learn how to speak with Him. There comes a point in our spiritual growth with Christ when it's not always a feeling but trust and faith. That's what I'm learning. I need to realize the Holy Spirit is with me, whether I "feel" Him or not. It isn't always easy, because you want to receive a sign, instead of walking by faith.

I'm officially tired of drinking juiced green peas. I've drunk the same juice for a long time. I shouldn't have bought so many of the same vegetables, but it's a lot cheaper when their bought in bulk. I feel great but miss the variety of juices I used to have. Thankfully, I'm almost out of green peas and I don't think I'm going to buy any more during this fast.

I'm still working on this last group project for Counseling Skills and my part of the presentation is on integrative psychotherapy. It has been challenging to say the least. I like this course, but there has been a huge course load and I'm ready for this semester to be over. I've enjoyed the role-play, learning micro skills, and becoming more knowledgeable on different types of counseling theories. As of now, I like Carl Rogers and his style. I also like existential therapy. In learning about counseling, I've also learned a lot about myself. As a counselor in training, I'm taking my education seriously—more seriously than ever. Putting the client's needs first has taught me about how to better interact with the people in my everyday life. This is one of the best times of my life. Thank You, Holy Spirit.

Day 78

Juice: *green peas, tomato, jalapeño, broccoli, avocado, green peppers*

Bible verses: *Job 5-6, Acts 5-6*

Behold, happy is the man whom God corrects; therefore do not despise the chastening of the Almighty. For He bruises, but he binds up; He wounds, but His hands make whole. He shall deliver you in six troubles, Yes, in seven no evil shall touch you. In famine He shall redeem you from death, And in war from the power of the sword. You shall be hidden from the scourge of the tongue, And you shall not be afraid of destruction when it comes. You shall laugh at destruction and famine, And you shall not be afraid of the beasts of the earth. For you shall have a covenant with the stones of the field, And the beasts of the field shall be at peace with you. You shall know that your tent is in peace; You shall visit your dwelling and finding nothing amiss. You shall also know that you descendants shall be many, And your offspring like the grass of the earth. You shall come to grave at full age, As a sheaf of grain ripens in its season. Behold, this we have searched out; It is true. Hear it, and know for yourself. Job 5:17-27

This Bible passage made itself prominent to me this morning. Job is being chastened by God but, even during the chastening, God is sharing with him how Job will be protected and will prosper. It makes me think about my own journey in life. Many times, I didn't know if God was with me even though He was. He has disciplined me, chastened me, but he has also made me successful at times. He is always with me through the Holy Spirit. The past month has been tough, but the Lord is with me and is strengthening me during these difficult times. He is showing me how to rest and let Him do the work. Through all of it, my faith has strengthened and I worship the Holy Spirit more than ever. Thank You, Holy Spirit, for the chastening. I know in due season, you will exalt me, because I endured through faith in you. In Jesus's name, Amen.

Day 79

Juice: green peas, tomato, jalapeño, broccoli, avocado, green peppers, radish, basil, parsley
Bible verses: Job 7-8, Acts 7-8

Finally! This is the last juice with green peas. They taste great, but I've been drinking green peas for too long.

I went to the grocery store and stocked up on fresh produce. I bought the same vegetables that I've been juicing, but add zucchini, cucumber, parsley, and basil. The fresh herbs taste great in the juice and give it an extra level of depth. I've been drinking avocados for almost this entire fast. I noticed I need the smoothness of the avocados to mask the grittiness of the other vegetables. They all blend well together to make a great juice. Tomorrow will be my first day adding the new produce to my juice mixes and I can't wait to taste the different flavors.

I made up my mind to buy my own scale. I don't know if I'm paranoid or if the scales are wrong at both the YMCAs where I work out. When I weigh myself at the Dowd YMCA, I'm 9 pounds heavier than at the other YMCA I work out at. I know my weight can fluctuate during a fast, but 9 pounds is a lot. From now on, I'm going to weigh myself at home and put one of my weights on the scale to make sure the scale is correct.

I notice that my midsection is shrinking and I can see more definition in my upper body. The midsection is the last to go. Since weighing myself the past couple of weeks, I've noticed my weight has fluctuated. I'm worried that I have plateaued, so I need to start stepping up my workouts. To break out of this plateau, I'm going to begin playing basketball again in the morning at the Dowd YMCA and add in cardio. Overall, I'm positive, feeling light, and I'm focused.

Day 80

Juice: *spinach, zucchini, cucumber, jalapeño, broccoli, radish, green pepper, green onion, avocado, parsley, basil*
Bible verses: *Job 9-10, Acts 9-10*

Twenty more days to go! Praise God! It has been an intense spiritual journey.

During the past week, I've had several lucid dreams. They have been intense, since I'm fighting demons and demonic people in my dreams. Fritz Perls, Laura Perls, and Paul Goodman developed Gestalt therapy, which is an existential form of psychotherapy. One technique is dream therapy. The client has to talk out the dream, repeat it, and make the dream come to life. In my dreams, I see myself fighting demons and demonic people whom I've never met. I've been waking up in the middle of the night in cold sweats, and then praying and casting out the demonic figures in Jesus's name.

I don't think it's a coincidence that I'm having these intense dreams during this fast. The enemy comes by thought first. The thought of temptation, anger, condemnation—these are all feelings that come as a thought first. The enemy sees me praising the Holy Spirit all day and thanking the Lord for all His blessings and lessons. But at night, when I'm sleeping, like a punk this clown named Satan wants to attack me. That's how this punk works. He waits until you are tired, hurt, broke, and desperate. Then he creeps in to steal, kill, and destroy. When the enemy comes, you need to say, "By the power and authority given to me by Jesus Christ, I command you, Satan, to get behind me and go back to hell. In Jesus's name, Amen!" He has to flee. God has given us the authority to trample Satan and his demonic army. Fight the Good fight! All day!

Your advisory is a relentless and loyal enemy. He will attack and attack. The more you praise God and fill yourself with the Holy Spirit, the more your temple is full and has no room for the enemy! Keep fighting the Good fight!

Thank you, Jesus, for your strength! Thank you for dying on the cross for me; thank you for giving me the power and authority to fight off the enemy. In Jesus's name, Amen!

Day 81

Juice: *spinach, zucchini, cucumber, jalapeño, broccoli, radish, green pepper, green onion, avocado, parsley, basil*
Bible verses: *Job 11-12, Acts 11-12*

I woke up late this morning. I guess my body needed the rest. I don't remember the last time I slept until 9 a.m. It has thrown me off this morning, because I do my writing, research, and papers in the morning. I enjoy doing my schoolwork in the morning, because I'm waking up out of a dream phase and waking up with clarity. The world hasn't gotten to me yet; the mornings are peaceful and still.

Finally, I make a juice without green peas. Today's juice tastes refreshing. I cut the zucchini into small bits along with the green onions. I like incorporating zucchini, because it helps in weight loss—so do cucumbers. I juice all of the vegetables first. When they are finished blending, I add fresh parsley and basil and blend it again. I like adding the herbs this way, because the juice of the vegetables is already made. To me, adding the herbs at the end enhances the flavor and I can always taste the herbs better.

Juicing is all about experimenting. I like to try new recipes and concoctions to make flavorful and healthy juices. I've made terrible juices in the past, when I first learned about juice fasting. I once juiced kale and spinach alone and gagged on the bitterness of the flavor. It was the worst juice I ever made. But I learned to start adding other fruits and vegetables to make the juices taste decent. Now, I love all the juices I make. After I'm finished with this hundred-day fast, I'm going to try out intermittent fasting for fifty days. I'll take a couple days off juicing and eat the foods I miss, but then I want to get back to it to see if intermittent fasting is a way of life I can consistently live with. I'm doing research now and I'm positive about it. I think the outcome will be awesome.

Today was a good day.

Day 82

Juice: spinach, zucchini, cucumber, jalapeño, broccoli, radish, green pepper, green onion, avocado, parsley, basil
Bible Verses: Job 13-14, Acts 13-14
Workout: lat pulldown, triceps, shoulder press, biceps, pec fly, row, incline press, swam 10 laps, 10 mins elliptical
Weight: 221.8 lb

I was really excited to work out this morning. I have a lot of energy and I haven't been to the gym for a while. I want to finish this fast strong and lose as much body fat as possible. When I've finished a fast in the past, I've always gained 5 to 7 pounds within that first week. I don't want to revert to old habits or put on any more excessive fat. I want to gain lean muscle and become even leaner. Gaining muscle mass will come, but I must stay consistent with my workouts. Lately, I haven't, because of my course load. But that's nothing more than an excuse as well.

I started my workout with ten minutes on the elliptical machine just to raise my heart rate. Then I went through my workout routine and noticed how much I was sweating. It felt good but I haven't sweated like that since the beginning of this fast. I can tell my body is plateauing and I need to counteract that.

I'm going to begin playing basketball in the moorings again at the Dowd YMCA. The games are intense and make for a good workout; plus, it will get me to do what I hate the most—which is running. I finished my workout with ten laps in the pool. It's my cool-down exercise and the water is a great place for me to meditate.

For the most part, I'm happy with today's workout. I'm prepping myself mentally to begin intense workouts on Monday and finish the last fourteen days of this fast strong.

Day 83

Juice: spinach, zucchini, cucumber, jalapeño, green pepper, green onion, avocado, parsley, basil

Bible verses: *Job 15-16, Acts 15-16*

My knee is killing me from yesterday's workout. It has been hurting all morning and it's that constant pain that doesn't go away. I feel good even though my knee hurts. I also feel light and notice more definition in my shoulders and arms. My midsection is losing more fat. The midsection is the last to go and I want to push myself to the edge to see results.

My friend, Mike, from the last marketing firm I worked at, asked me to lunch today. I've been dodging him for lunch because of this fast, but when I finally told him I was fasting, he understood. I agreed to have lunch with him, however, thinking it'd be a great opportunity to cook for him and share my testimony with him. I told him I wasn't going to eat. Instead, I would cook for him. Mike is huge fan of cheeseburgers, just like me, so I prepped for him a bison burger. Bison is a great, red meat, which has a sweeter taste than beef. It's also really healthy and a lean protein. I also made the bread and put a bunch of parsley and basil into it. I used many of the vegetables I juice, like tomatoes, zucchini, green peppers, and green onion, and made a savory spread.

I met Mike uptown—his job is next to Montreat College and I run into him all the time. It was good to sit and talk with him about many topics, like work, school, my fast, and good, healthy guy talk. I was happy to see his expression after taking a bite of the bison burger. He loved it. It was good to catch up with him and see that he's doing well.

I didn't work out today, but I had a great time explaining my testimony to a good friend. Balance is the key to life.

Day 84

Juice: spinach, zucchini, jalapeño, green pepper, green onion, avocado, parsley, basil

Bible verses: Job 17-18, Acts 17-18

In the book of Acts, chapter 18, Paul leaves Athens and travels to Corinth. He is to spread the word that Jesus is the Christ. He meets a Jew named Aquila and Aquila's wife, Pricilla. They arrived in Corinth, because all of the Jews were cast out of Rome. Paul stays with them, since they have the same beliefs. They were of the same trade as tentmakers. Every Sabbath, Paul would go to the synagogue and proclaim his faith to the Jews and to the Greeks. Many of them converted and became followers of Jesus Christ. However, some blasphemed him and opposed him, but Paul stayed strong.

> *Your blood be upon your own heads; I am clean. From now on I will go to the Gentiles. Acts 18:6*

This story jumped out at me, because when we share our testimony and people are not receptive, you have to let it go and let God take over. Christians will not win everyone over to Christ and it isn't our job to force Jesus on them. We are to share our testimony and if it leads a person to Christ, great. If not, we're supposed to let go and let God. So many Christians fail to realize "you" are not winning them over. God is.

The Lord spoke to Paul in the night by a vision.

> *Do not be afraid, but speak, and do not keep silent; For I am with you, and no one will attack you to hurt you; for I have many people in the city. Acts 18:9-10*

We are too bold with our faith without being boastful or prideful. Instead, we should be humble and genuine. The only way I can speak about my walk is by speaking about my hurts and hang-ups, and how I had failed and turned to Jesus. I challenge everyone who follows Christ to share your testimony through a humble heart.

Day 85

Juice: *spinach, cucumber, avocado, zucchini, green pepper, green onion*
Bible verses: *Job 19-20, Acts 19-20*
Workout: *2.5-mile run*

I went to the 11 a.m. church service this morning and it felt great to worship the Lord, since I did not attend church last week. The songs we sang spoke to me and the Holy Spirit's presence was in the sanctuary. Pastor Eli preached on Remembrance in Revelation 3:3 and the message was excellent.

> *"Remember therefore how you have received and heard; hold fast and repent. Therefore if you will not watch, I will come upon you as a thief, and you will not know what hour I will come upon you."*

Pastor Eli said that the Bible speaks of the call to remember more than the call to pray or the call to forgive. The passage in Revelation speaks about remembering who Jesus Christ is and who he is in our life. In our relationship with God, we must put nothing before Him.

So many Christians are just Christians on Sunday morning. That isn't having a relationship with Jesus Christ; that is more of a hobby. God knows our heart—who is genuine and who isn't. We can't fool God and we shouldn't even try. All we're doing is making fools of ourselves. The message today really hit home. Even though I'm fasting, I read my Bible, and I have a relationship with the Holy Spirit, I'm lacking in growth through my church. I'm going to make a commitment today to get involved. I'm going to volunteer through my church and be more involved in growing the congregation.

I did run into friends, Andre and Diane, who are sponsoring a small group on praying. I am going to join their group on Thursday evenings and delve deeper into prayer. I'm going to email Pastor Chad this week and let him know I want to get more involved. I'm glad I went to church today and heard that message. I believe God is speaking to me.

Today, at 3 p.m., I felt like running. I haven't run outside on a trail in over a year, but I've been thinking about running or playing basketball again. I can tell my body is plateauing in weight loss, so I need to recharge my workout. I want to add in intense cardio, so I've decided to drive to the greenway and go for a run. Where I begin at the greenway, it's a downhill run for the first quarter of a mile. I think this helps me begin the motion of running. I didn't know how far I was going to run, but I ran to a 1.25-mile marker, turned around, and then ran the rest. It might not have been pretty, but I made it without stopping.

I listened to Christian podcasts and meditated while on my run. I kept saying to myself, "Each step is a blessing." I repeated it over and over, and kept my head down, continuously pumping my arms, until I made it to where I began.

It felt good to run. My legs were like Jell-O when I was finished, but it was well worth it. I'm going to try to run every day for the rest of this fast. I want to prove to myself that I can finish strong even when I'm tired.

Day 86

Juice: spinach, kale, jalapeño, cucumber, avocado, zucchini, green pepper, green onion
Bible verses: Job 21-22, Acts 21-22
Workout: 2.5-mile run, bench press, isolateral chest press, shoulder shrugs, row/rear deltoid, lat pull-down
Weight: 220.8 lb, 66.7lb loss

Today, I committed a cardinal sin when it came to working out. I ran long distance and then lifted weights. I don't care. I felt energized after running and I wanted to lift weights. I only did one set of burnouts, but I wanted to push my body and my mind to the limit this morning.

After working out, I went home and looked into my full-length mirror. Even though I'm happy with my results, I'm at the stage where I have that stubborn visceral fat in my midsection, which is holding on for dear life. I immediately begin to research ways to burn visceral fat and how to get to the next level in my gains.

I come across a few articles on jumping rope. Is jumping rope better than running? That's the question I want answered. I go onto YouTube and look up the training guru, Big Brandon Carter. If you don't know who he is, look him up. He's a huge shredded man, who makes YouTube videos on lifting, working out, and supplements—everything that has to do with healthy living. He has a raw personality but is highly knowledgeable when it comes to fitness. In his videos, he shares how to run sprints after working out and how jump roping can help burn fat.

After watching a few of his videos and some others, I immediately searched for my jump rope in my closet. Before class, I went to the gym in my apartment complex and began to jump rope. I thought I was going to die after thirty seconds. I had to remember how to jump rope again. Once I finally got into a routine, I began jumping rope for thirty seconds. Then I'd do crunches on a fitness ball. I repeated that for about three minutes and then began jumping rope for one minute with intervals of crunches. When

I was finished with the workout, I was completely drained. I only jumped rope for five minutes, but it was a killer workout.

Today is a perfect lesson in life. We're not always going to see gains spiritually, in health, or in our careers by doing the same thing all the time. Sometimes, we have to step it up and reach another level of intestinal fortitude to reach the gains we want to see. When I woke up this morning I had no clue jumping rope would be a part of my daily routine. This fast is me saying to God, "I want to go to another level of spirituality and grow my relationship with You." I want God to know I am honoring Him through mind, body, soul, and my spirit. I want to prove to myself, through the Holy Spirit, I can do anything I set my mind and heart on

Day 87

Juice: kale, spinach, tomato, jalapeño, green pepper, zucchini, cucumber, avocado

Bible verses: Job 23-24, Acts 23-24

Workout: 5 min interval jump rope, bench press, incline press, decline press, shoulder press, mid row, seated dips, 10 40-yd sprints

Wow, I can see a difference in jumping rope already. I went to my apartment gym and jumped rope for five minutes with intervals of crunches. I felt great getting my heart rate up in the morning after waking up. My rest was the drive to the YMCA, where I lifted, felt loose, and decided to do sprints when I was finished. I haven't sprinted in a long time and my only concern was pulling a muscle in my legs. For the first sprint, I took off as fast as I could and while I was running, I remember looking at comparisons between a long-distance runner's body and a sprinter's body. A long-distance runner's body is thin and frail, while a sprinter's body is muscular and shredded. I want a sprinter's body. I ran ten sprints and I was exhausted when I finished. It's amazing to see how much my body has changed in eighty-seven days.

I love working out now and it reminds me of how we can change the way we think when we change our perspective. I was tired of being fat and overweight. I didn't like the way I felt and wasn't as happy or energetic. Now, I love waking up in the mornings and beginning my day with the same rituals of praying, reading my Bible, and meditating on worshiping God. However, after my spiritual rituals, I hit the gym immediately and I'm not quick to work out and leave. I take my time working out and focused on the body parts I am training. I've grown a lot during this fast and I'm so thankful that the Lord led me to do this.

I feel great today and I am happy.

Day 88

Juice: *kale, spinach, cucumber, zucchini, green pepper, jalapeño, avocado, parsley*
Bible verses: *Job 25-26, Acts 25-26*
Workout: *10 min interval jump rope, ab crunches, squats, leg curls, leg extension, 10 swim laps*

Our bodies are designed to adapt and adapt quickly. I'm astonished at how quickly my body has adapted to jumping rope in such a short time. It has been years since I last jumped rope and today, I was able to jump rope for ten minutes of interval training. It felt great. I did it prior to my workout and I felt a difference in how I was able to lift weights. My body felt loose, I had a lot of energy, and I was able to focus on the body parts I was lifting. I definitely recommend adding jumping rope to your workout. After that workout, I was tired for the rest of the day. I pushed my body hard today and I can tell I'm going to need to rest soon.

Jesus said to Paul:

> *But rise and stand on your feet; for I have appeared to you for this purpose, to make you a minister and a witness both of the things which you have seen and of the things which I will yet reveal to you. Acts 26:16*

I love this scripture, because what Jesus says to Paul is how we are to speak of our Christian faith. We are to be a witness of the things we have gone through and how we have come to be followers of Jesus Christ. When I recommitted my life in December 2011, I did it at the church I was attending in Austin, in front of my grandparents and my mother and sister. It was the day after I graduated from college. I made a public dedication in front of my church. My grandfather spoke afterward. He explained me as a "tough piece of meat that needs to be tenderized." I thought that was a perfect way to explain myself, because I was a new follower; I still made many mistakes and would condemn myself all the time. Also, my personality at the time was still rough and tough from serving eight years in the army and two tours to Iraq. My heart was not tenderized to the Holy Spirit and to the ways of Jesus Christ. Looking back on it now, there were a lot of tough times growing in Christ. I would still party, go to bars, do drugs, and chase women. However, I would always repent and try to live righteously. God knows our heart, even when we sin. When I see how much I have grown, it's astonishing to know that the Lord is using me to explain to non-believers and to believers that who we are in Jesus Christ is perfect in His eyes. Just because a person begins to follow Christ does not mean their walk is going to change overnight. It has taken me several years to become the man I am today. Through relentless prayer and studying the word of God, I have changed my ways. But that transition is needed to build our faith.

> *For a righteous man may fall seven times*
> *And rise again,*
> *But the wicked shall fall by calamity. Proverbs 24:16*

The Lord knows we are going to make mistakes along our walk with Him and we are called to be a witness of how He changes our lives. Never in a million years did I think I would be writing a book about a spiritual fast, about Jesus Christ, and my walk with Him. I'm confident the majority of the people from my past will be shocked as well. I know I will never be perfect and I know I will make mistakes, but God's mercy is new every morning. I strive daily to be a righteous man.

Day 89

Juice: spinach, kale, green onion, green pepper, jalapeño, avocado, parsley, basil
Bible verses: Job 27-28, Acts 27-28
Workout: 10 min interval jump rope, biceps, triceps, pec fly, seated dips, shoulder press, lat raise

I woke up motivated to grab my jump rope and begin training this morning. I'm focused on my body, my temple, and turning it into the healthiest temple I can. I haven't been this motivated in my life when it comes to my health. I don't want to be overweight ever again. I want to be in the greatest shape of my life. When people look at me, I want them to see a fit man of God, who looks like David—a warrior.

My confidence is growing every day and as I research fitness and health, I see how many mistakes I've made and the lack of discipline I've demonstrated for so many years. Even though I'm not married or have children, I'm getting in shape for them as well. I want to be that dad who is in great shape. I want to be that middle-aged man one day, who can keep up with the youngsters. Thinking about these future events puts a smile on my face, because I'm speaking it into existence and I will live that lifestyle.

After my workout, I diligently completed my last research paper for Counseling Skills. I have one week left and have to take a final for this course. It feels great to have accomplished so much during this course. This course has been challenging since day one. During this semester, my grandfather passed away, but I didn't miss one class. I dealt with it the best I could and God's anointment has been with me the entire time. Thank You, Father, for challenging me during this semester. It has been tough, but my faith in You grew. I'm so thankful for the breakthrough I've had spiritually and physically during this fast. I never would have thought in a million years that I would be doing a spiritual fast.

Day 90

Juice: spinach, kale, tomato, green pepper, green onion, jalapeño, avocado, zucchini, cucumber, basil

Bible verses: Job 29-30, Hebrews 1-2

I love the book of Hebrews. It is one of my favorite books in the Bible.

> *God who at various times and in various ways spoke in time past to the fathers by the prophets, has in these last days spoken to us by His Son, whom He has appointed heir of all things, through whom also He made the worlds. Hebrews 1:1-2*

This is God's supreme revelation of His son, Jesus Christ. Since Jesus is the heir of the throne, and followers of Jesus Christ are considered his children, that would make us royalty. What an amazing way to view our relationship with Jesus. As a believer of Jesus Christ, I have royal blood pumping through my veins. I've spoken this to my siblings and as humbly as I can, view myself as royalty. Jesus Christ, my spiritual father, is the ruler over all things and I am one of His sons. Since Jesus Christ is my spiritual father, I inherit His kingdom when I die and go to heaven. This alone gives me peace about death. So many people fear death, but when you have a relationship with your spiritual father, it should give you peace about the afterlife.

Considering one's self to be royalty should make one live out their life with integrity and good character. We all make mistakes, but we repent and keep moving forward. We are called to be quick to forgive, show mercy, and, above all things, show love. If we can just do those three things, we can live a life of good character.

Each day, I'm trying to grow in my spirit and strengthen my relationship with the Holy Spirit. I've learned that sometimes the best option is to be quiet. When I become angry with people or I witness immoral behavior, instead of saying something that can be hurtful or offensive, sometimes it's best to shut up and let God do the talking for me. It is easier said than done, but I'm learning.

Day **91**

Juice: tomato, green onion, green pepper, jalapeño, avocado, basil, cucumber

Bible verses: Job 31-32, Hebrews 3-4

Workout: 10 min interval jump rope, dumbbell bench press, dumbbell incline press, kneeling one arm row, biceps, shadowboxing with weights, swam 10 laps

Today's workout was awesome. I used dumbbells to work out my chest, instead of using a straight bar. It seemed to be a better workout and I worked out until I had muscle failure. I also incorporated shadowboxing with five-pound weights. I used a lot of upper body muscles that I never realized I had.

When I woke up this morning, I didn't feel like working out, but I pushed myself to go to the gym and I'm glad I did. Even though I had a great workout, I have become distraught with my weight loss. It seems like I've completely plateaued and can't lose any more weight. I don't know if it's because I'm gaining muscle that it seems like I haven't lost any more weight, but it's become an issue.

I have to be careful with pushing myself, because lately, I'm hungry by the end of the day. I can tell my body is craving food. I'm now making two juices a day: I drink one in the morning after my workout and then I make another juice in the afternoon. I'm shocked that I haven't become tired of the juices, since I make the same one almost every day. I've noticed that if I don't add jalapeño or avocado to the recipe, I don't like it as much. I like the smooth and spicy flavor they both add. I've been adding both to my juices for a long time.

I wonder how my body is going to react when I begin to eat solid foods again. I've been craving a cheeseburger for a couple of days now and I keep envisioning eating my favorite foods when I'm finished with this fast. I have nine days left and it seems like the days are dragging. I'm excited, because completing this fast is going to be one of my proudest moments, but these last days have become torturous. I want it to be over soon.

Day 92

Juice: spinach, green and red peppers, cucumber, zucchini, jalapeño, avocado, tomato, green onion
Bible verses: Job 33-34, Hebrews 5-6
Workout: 1.5 mile run

I was excited to attend church this morning. I want to worship God and hear the message that will strengthen me for this last week of my fast.

We had a guest speaker and he spoke about being a good neighbor and what that means as a follower of Christ. It was a great message and I had a great time of worship. In Job 33, it states, "The Spirit of God has made me, And the breath of the Almighty gives me life." This is powerful and true and resonates with how I feel today.

Regularly attending church is my life force. It strengthens me and is a time for me to strengthen my relationship with God. I love my church's contemporary service and I can relate to the music and sermons. I've become less worried about the people around me when I'm worshiping God and lifting my hands in the air. I used to be too worried about what other people thought and I wouldn't fully worship the Lord. This fast has taught me to trust God and not worry about what others think of me. As long as I'm in good standing with the Lord, everything else will fall into place.

After the service, I decide to go for a run at the greenway. I'm not going to go for a long run, but it's a good time for me to meditate with the Lord and clear my head. I've also learned what a runner's high is and I really like that feeling. To me, it feels like my mind is completely clear, I'm calm and I'm at peace. It's a great feeling and I believe I need that to begin this week, take my final for Counseling Skills, and to complete the last week of this fast.

Day 93

Juice: spinach, green and red peppers, cucumber, zucchini, jalapeño, avocado, tomato, green onion
Bible verses: Job 35-36, Hebrews 7-8
Workout: 10 min interval jump rope, dumbbell bench press, dumbbell incline press, kneeling one arm row, biceps, shadowboxing with weights, swam 10 laps
Weight: 223.4 lb, 64.1 lb loss

This morning, I woke up and immediately weighed myself. I weigh 223.4 pounds and I've gained a few pounds since last week. I'm not discouraged like I was earlier, because I've been working out hard and I'm sure the weight gain is due to an increase in muscle mass. I'm not as concerned about my weight as I am with fat loss. I feel great. My midsection is slowly but surely burning off and I have a lot of energy in the weight room at the gym. I've also begun taking creatine monohydrate. From the studies I have read, creatine is a great product for muscle gain.

My body is sore but in a good way. My calves have been burning since jumping rope. Since I've incorporated shadowboxing with five-pound weights, I can feel muscle fatigue in my upper back and shoulders. The feeling I get from training is a good feeling and I know the soreness will eventually go away when my body becomes acclimated to my new lifestyle. That's exactly what this has become—a lifestyle.

Now, I love waking up to go to the gym. While I'm working out, it's a great time to reflect on how I envision my day going. Today, I'm thinking about my final for Counseling Skills. I'm so happy this class is finally over. I learned a lot but, at times, the workload was overwhelming. My cohort feels the same way. We're all ready to move on from this class and begin our next course, which is Spirituality and Religion in Counseling. It should be interesting and we're all excited to begin another course.

What a difference a year makes. I've almost completed my first year training as a counselor in a graduate program; I've met some great people here in Charlotte; I have a great dog; and I'm fasting for a hundred days. Life is awesome.

Today, I'm really counting my blessings and reflecting on this journey. God's hand has been on me the entire time. During the good and the bad, the Lord has been steering me to be the man I am today. I am so thankful for all of the people in my life and the ones who have passed through. Lately, I've been praying for the people of my past—even if we either had a falling out, moved on, or whatever be the reason. All of them have shown me something about myself and how I want to live my life. Thank You, Holy Spirit, for all of the people who have passed through my life. Thank You for all of the leaders I've had. Thank You for all of the friends I've had. Thank You for my teachers, professors, coaches, and mentors. I pray You bless every single person I have had a relationship with. Bless them and their families and show them mercy, grace, and love. In Jesus's name, Amen.

Day 94

Juice: spinach, green and red pepper, cucumber, zucchini, jalapeño, avocado, tomato, green onion, basil

Bible verses: Job 37-38, Hebrews 9-10

Workout: 5 min interval jump rope, squat, leg curls, leg extension, swam 10 laps

A subtitle in Hebrews 10 is Hold Fast Your Confession:

> *Let us draw near with a true heart in full assurance of faith, having our hearts sprinkled from an evil conscience and our bodies washed with pure water. Let us hold fast the confession of our hope without wavering, for He who promised is faithful. And let us consider one another in order to stir up love and good works, not forsaking the assembling of ourselves together, as is the manner of some, but exhorting one another, and so much the more as you see the Day approaching. Hebrews 10:19-25*

God is faithful and, as a believer, I need to remember God's plan is better than my plan. God's timing is better than my timing. God's favor is sufficient. His love and plan for my life is going to be better than I could ever expect. Time after time, God has blessed me and anointed me for that period of my life. In so many instances, I know it was not me alone but God's anointing of me.

Today, I had a job interview to be a caregiver for senior citizens. My interview went great and the hiring director looked over my resume and said to me, "Ulysses, you have accomplished a lot in life." I was offered the position and will begin training in two weeks. Finally, my first job in the health care field. The hiring director really liked that I'm a veteran. She explained to me that there a lot of senior citizen veterans who are lonely and she wants me to work specifically with them.

God sometimes uses our situations to prepare us for our journey in life. Last month, I was helping my grandfather—a Korean war veteran—while he was on his death bed. Now, I'm going to help other veterans. I can't ask for a better situation. Thank you, Jesus. God's anointment and favor have been with me on this journey. Even when I backslid and didn't have a relationship with God, He was still there, exalting me. What an awesome God I serve. He blessed me even when I turned my back on Him. He blessed me during the drunken nights. He blessed me during the drugs, the sex, the anger, and the hurt. God blessed me. He blesses me daily. It's reassuring to know I serve a God who shows me unconditional love.

Day 95

Juice: *spinach, green pepper, red pepper, cucumber, zucchini, jalapeño, avocado, tomato, green onion, basil*
Bible verses: *Job 39-40, Hebrews 11-12*
Workout: *10-min interval run, swam 10 laps, 10-min interval jump rope*

The anxiety of completing this fast has grown during this last week. I'm ready to complete this mission and be free to eat food again. It's crazy that it's day 95. I'm the one going through this fast and I can barely believe this journey. In some ways, this fast has gone by rather quickly, but I remember how much of an emotional rollercoaster this journey has been. I can't believe it's almost over. I have accomplished a lot in life, but this one will stand out the most to me.

I dedicated one hundred days to God by breaking away from the world and fasting. I have tried to honor God throughout this journey and envision how this fast will impact the rest of my life. I don't really know what to think of it all. I've written down all of the reasons I'm fasting and I don't know if God will honor all of the prayers on that list. I do know, however, my relationship with the Holy Spirit has grown by leaps and bounds.

This fast has become such a big part of who I am, that I don't know what it's going to be like to eat food again. I'm so conditioned not to worry about eating that I have no idea what type of effect it has had on me. I still do not understand why God called me to fast for one hundred days. I might not ever know the answer. Maybe it was just to bring me to a higher level, spiritually.

I know I have relied on the Lord. My relationship with Him has strengthened and, mentally and physically, I am at peace and happy. Right now, I feel content even though I know there will be people who criticize me or don't believe this hundred-day journey. I've made my peace with that and I'm not worried about defending myself. I trust God will protect me and keep my enemies away from me. I know God is with me.

Day 96

Juice: spinach, green and red peppers, cucumber, zucchini, jalapeño, avocado, tomato, green onion, basil
Bible verses: Job 41-42, Hebrews 13
Workout: 3 min interval jump rope, 3 min shadowboxing with 5-lb weights, chest press, pulldown, low/rear deltoid, shoulder press, triceps, biceps, shoulder shrugs, swam 10 laps

It feels like my soul wants to jump out of my flesh. I'm close to insanity and want this week to end.

I had a great workout, but I've made up my mind that today will be the last day I lift weights until this fast is over. Hunger has crept back into my life and I'm confident it has to do with my workouts. All I can think about is eating a sandwich or a cheeseburger—living a normal life which consists of *food*. I've become emotional lately, either with anger or with anxiety.

I still feel like a fool at times for thinking this fast matters. Who does it matter to? Does God really care I've fasted for ninety-six days? Does my family? I don't even know if I care anymore. It might just be that I'm so close to the finish line, that I can't give up now. I've become depressed, I don't know what it's like for a person to deal with postpartum depression, but somehow, that's the only way I know how I can relate when looking up the definition. I have a lot of anxiety and I don't know why. I wish I could talk to my grandpa about this kind of stuff but he's dead. I hate that I have to figure things out by solely relying on God. It isn't always easy to have faith and today is one of those days. The days are becoming long and drawn out even though I'm so close to finishing this fast. I'm going to watch Netflix the rest of the day and hopefully, fall asleep early.

Day 97

Juice: *spinach, green and red peppers, cucumber, zucchini, jalapeño, avocado, tomato*
Bible verses: *First book of Peter, second book of Peter*
Workout: *1 mile run, 1mile walk, swam 20 laps*

This fast is in my head now and all I can think about is finishing it. I don't feel any better since yesterday. The closer I am to finishing this fast, the crazier I feel. I just want it all to end. I'm trying to find things to do, but all I really want to do is sleep. I want to sleep until the morning so another day is over. Now, I only have three days left.

I know I'm going to begin intermittent fasting when this fast is over, so I began researching about it. The best times to eat during intermittent fasting is right after a workout. I work out in the mornings, so my window for eating will be from 8 a.m. to 1 p.m. From 1 p.m. onward, I'll fast until 8 a.m. the next day. I'll begin eating this way and I've decided to go to the butcher shop and pick up high-quality proteins. I bought boneless goat, lamb, and chicken. I made a marinade for the proteins and chopped up a bunch of vegetables. My plan is to combine the vegetables and protein and, on the eve of 4th of July, put it all in a crock-pot and cook it overnight. That way, when I wake up on July 5th, I will have a high-quality-protein meal to begin my intermittent fasting.

I was going to go to the beach for 4th of July and have my first meal there, but I received a phone call from the Myrtle Beach State Park. They informed me that the 4th of July is busy and, since I'm checking in that day, I should wait until the afternoon to arrive. That call let me know I shouldn't go; I should stay in Charlotte, wake up on the 5th, and eat a high-protein meal. Prepping the proteins and vegetables took a lot of time and I became tired early.

I fell asleep around 8:30pm the last two evenings and woke up around 5 a.m. I'm fine with that. I just want to eat again and live a normal life. I pray I stay strong for the next couple of days and that I have self-control to not let my emotions get to me.

Day 98

Juice: spinach, green and red peppers, cucumber, zucchini, jalapeño, avocado, tomato
Bible verses: *First book of John, Second book of John, Third book of John*

The three books of John are about love and how love represents who God is. God is love. God is light and God is life. John explains this through these books and reiterates that a follower of Christ represents His love.

Lately, I've been praying for my enemies and the people who are no longer a part of my life. Sometimes, it's hard to pray for them, because I honestly don't want God to bless them. But I know that's my flesh, not my spirit. As I grow closer to God, I'm learning to pray for my enemies so they can hopefully begin a relationship with God. Expressing unconditional love is a challenge. I believe it is a life-long journey to becoming a loving person toward the people who have hurt us.

One of my morning rituals is to take Top for a walk. I pray for family, friends, and now enemies, during our walk. When I pray for my enemies, I ask the Lord to show them mercy and grace. I ask the Lord to remove the confusion from their hearts and minds. I pray the Lord reveals Himself to them and they take steps to begin a relationship with Him. Years ago, I would never pray for my enemies. Well, at least, not positive prayers. I would have prayed for the Lord to kill my enemies.

Spiritual growth is real. I'm an example of the fact that God can use anyone. I pray that my story—my testimony—touches someone's heart and they begin a relationship with God. God is love and He has shown me love all of my life. I'm happy today and happy this fast is almost complete. I've learned so much about myself and what I'm capable of. I've also learned to really rely on God. My faith is strengthening daily. I strive to be a beacon of light in this dark world.

Today was a great day.

Day 99

Juice: *spinach, green and red peppers, cucumber, zucchini, jalapeño, avocado, tomato*

Bible verses: *First book of Thessalonians, Second book of Thessalonians*

The way I feel right now is indescribable. I can't believe it's day ninety-nine and I only have one more day of fasting left. This has been an incredible journey and I would not have grown my relationship with the Holy Spirit the way I did without this fast. I'm so thankful the Lord led me to it. I feel blessed to have been called to partake on a journey with my spiritual father. I learned a lot about who I am, who I'm not, and who I want to become. My faith has been tested many times during this fast, but I stuck it out and my faith grew stronger. The Lord wouldn't have led me to this fast if he didn't think I could handle the pressure. As a man of God, I am called to pick up my cross and follow him. I believe this is me picking up my cross and following Him on this fasting journey.

My attitude has become a little erratic. The anxiety of completing this task is overwhelming. However, I find myself having bursts of joy and becoming emotionally thankful for this experience. I've confined myself to my apartment and I've closed myself off to the outside world. I have spent the day in meditation, watching Netflix, and praying. At times, I fall asleep. My lucid dreams envision my future and how this fast will affect my life and my family's life for generations to come.

God has called me to fast to break the cycle in my family. What an honor. Thank You, Father, for this task, this journey, and strengthening my relationship with You.

Day 100

Juice: spinach, tomato, jalapeño, avocado, cucumber, zucchini
Bible verses: The Book of James
Weight: 223 lb, 64.5 lb loss

Today is the last day of this fast and I'm constantly looking at the clock. I find it funny that I'm counting down the hours and I'm in good spirits. It doesn't matter to me that it's the 4th of July. I have purposely shut myself off from the world and do not plan on leaving my apartment all day or night. I don't care about fireworks. I don't care about missing out on barbecuing—none of that stuff matters to me. All that matters is my relationship with the Holy Spirit and being fed by Him. The Holy Spirit has fed me during this fast. At times, I didn't realize it but, since day 1 of this fast, I see how much I've grown and how my relationship has grown with the Holy Spirit.

Every morning since Pentecost Sunday, I've taken Top for a walk, praising and worshiping the Holy Spirit with each step. I pray to the Holy Spirit. I talk to the Holy Spirit and I am fed by the Holy Spirit. I feel so strong, emotionally and spiritually. I feel like a warrior who awaits battle. I want the battle; I welcome the battle; and I am prosperous in the spiritual fight. I will always win the spiritual battle, because I am a man filled with the goodness of the Holy Spirit. Christ is with me and so is the hope for glory. I am favored in spiritual battle; I am favored in love; I am favored in success; I am favored in prosperity; I am favored in success; I am favored in all walks of my life and I am anointed to fulfill my mission for the Kingdom of God. No one on this planet has the power or the authority to stop God's plan for my life. No one on this planet has the power or the authority to stop God's anointing of my life. My anointing is refreshed, recharged, and renewed. I am a Beacon of Light for the Kingdom of God. Jesus Christ is my Lord, my savior. I will worship Him. My family will worship Him. I will exalt His name at all times. No weapon will prosper against me or my family. Jesus Christ has given me the power and the authority to speak greatness into my life; He has given me the power and authority to speak healing into my life; He has given me the power and authority to walk as he walked. I will fulfill God's plan and nobody will stop me.

I feel God's supernatural power and my confidence overflows. I don't feel weak; instead I am stronger than ever. I know now that I did not sacrifice anything on this fast. Instead, I gained the power of the Holy Spirit. As this fast comes to an end, I contemplate on all of my accomplishments and successes. This hundred-day fast is the greatest accomplishment of my life. No one can take away the power, love, and Christ-like wisdom I have gained through this fast. Thank You, Holy Spirit, for feeding me during these hundred days. I will love and honor You until the day I die.

But if serving the LORD seems undesirable to you, then choose for yourselves this day whom you will serve, whether the gods your ancestors served beyond the Euphrates, or the gods of the Amorites, in whose land you are living. But as for me and my household, we will serve the LORD. Joshua 24:15